School(s) for Conversion:
12 Marks of a
New Monasticism

edited by

The Rutba House

Cascade Books
A division of *Wipf & Stock Publishers*
199 West 8th Avenue, Suite 3 • Eugene OR 97401

Cascade Books
A division of Wipf & Stock Publishers
199 West 8th Avenue, Suite 3
Eugene, OR 97401

School(s) for Conversion:
12 Marks of a New Monasticism
Copyright©2005 by The Rutba House
ISBN: 1-59752-055-1
Publication Date: February 2005

10   9   8   7   6   5   4   3   2   1

For Clint and Darshan Hartgrove,
Mary Jo Haw,
Marti Wilson,
and Leah Wilson-Hartgrove,
who served so a conversation could happen.

Table of Contents

Editors' Preface

The Rutba House

As far as we know, this is the first book edited by a house. The Rutba House is a Christian community of hospitality, peacemaking, and discipleship. We are shaped by our common life and rule for living. We pray together daily, share meals, fast once a week, and worship together as a way of shaping our life around the gospel. These are important practices that form our identity as we try to be faithful disciples of Jesus. But it is our neighbors who ground the Rutba House and help us remember who we are.

Ms. Nora comes to dinner, bringing her signature potato salad or collard greens; Frank and William stop by on the weekends to play with our dog Stanley and yell in our high-ceiling house; Carolyn and Wallace join us for Bible study. Others we have come to love through worship at Northside Baptist Church and St. John's Baptist Church in our neighborhood. We are formed by these people, our neighbors. They have become a part of us and we have become a part of them—our stories are bound together. Sharing life with them has changed how we think about the future and how we reflect on our past. They have challenged our life as a "radical" community. And they have taught us how important it is to remain connected to our past and to recognize the faithfulness that already exists in this place.

So we have watched and learned from the good work God is doing in a neighborhood where folks like us "aren't supposed to live." We watched our church respond to a murder in the neighborhood with prayer walks and vigils; we have seen senior citizens take care of other senior citizens; and we have witnessed the persistent prayers of saints who have stayed put and kept the faith through the years. In a place that real estate agents and city planners think worthless, we've found a pearl of great price. And so the question: why *wouldn't* Christians want to be in a place like this? Why wouldn't the church who finds her identity in a history of exodus and exile, in the story of a Refugee who was executed by an Empire and resurrected by the King of the universe, want to be where God has been active all along—on the margins and in the abandoned places?

When we started the Rutba House in the summer of 2003, we tried to listen closely to a wide network of Christians who were asking these kinds of questions and experimenting with forms of community and discipleship. The Catholic Worker tradition offered a vision of hospitality houses in the cities and "agronomic universities" on the land—a society, as Peter Maurin had said, in which it would be easier for people to be good. The Christian Community Development Association (CCDA) promised multiethnic inner-city communities characterized by John Perkins' three "Rs": relocation, redistribution, and reconciliation. Friends in the Emergent Fellowship criticized the church's marriage to modernity and asked how an "ancient/future" faith might produce a "new kind of Christian." Mentors from the RENOVARE movement taught us to drink deep from the "streams of living water" that still flow through the spiritual classics and the ancient practices of the church. Theologians and pastors from the Ekklesia Project talked about the church as a counter-culture that God has gifted with time for peace in this peculiar place called America.

As we read the Bible together and asked what it would mean to live the way of Jesus in our neighborhood, we met others who were asking the same question. The Bruderhof invited us to learn from their 60 years of experience in communities of radical discipleship. We met people from the Shalom Mission Network, Atlantic Life Community, Antioch Communities and other associations of Christians living in intentional community. Others we met were not part of any larger network. They had started communities out of Bible studies in their churches and neighborhood-safety meetings in their housing projects; with fellow students on their college campuses and recovering addicts in the inner-city.

Some of our friends in the church warned us of the dangers of community living. We heard stories of communes in the 60s and 70s that had started with lofty ideals only to later become destructive. Others expressed hope that we would become more realistic and "settle down." We listened carefully to these critical voices. Jesus did, after all, tell his disciples that before following him they should count the cost. But he also called them to leave everything and follow him. We took seriously the warnings from our friends, but we also knew God had called us to this adventure. What we needed was a way to understand radical discipleship as a faithful expression of the best in the church's long tradition.

Studying church history helped. As we looked together at the long sweep of the church's story (as an extension of Israel's story), we began to see that the church's response to compromise and crisis has consistently been one of new monastic movements. When the emperors made Christianity legal and offered the favors of their Empire in the 4th century, the Desert Fathers and Mothers began the first monastic movement by fleeing the centers of power and creating alternative communities in the desert. In the midst of the Crusades, as religious violence raged, St. Francis rejected economic privilege and started a new monastic movement.

Not all monastic movements were within the Roman Catholic communion. The Anabaptists of the 16th century sought to establish a community of authentic Christian witness over and against the corrupt state churches of Europe. Likewise, slaves in the United States cultivated a liberation theology and tradition of subversive song in the underground churches of "Christian" plantations. In an age when "Christian" America is the "last remaining superpower" in an all-out "war on terror," we've begun to think that once again it is time for a new monasticism. Indeed, this is how we see the Spirit moving in North America today.

So in June 2004, with the help of a generous grant from the Fund for Theological Education, we invited friends from around the country to come to Durham and help us discern a possible shape of a new monasticism. Those gathered discerned twelve marks that may help communicate common characteristics of these diverse communities. Some marks are more visible in some communities than others, yet all recognize the work of the Holy Spirit in their common forms of life sketched in the twelve marks. The list is not to be understood as the necessary shape of all faithful witness. Rather, it helps name the unique witness these neo-monastic communities have to offer the rest of the church.

The essays in this book give more texture to the twelve marks by rooting the convictions in our Scriptures and the history of the church, and providing stories that display the kinds of faithfulness the marks describe. The authors share from their storehouses of wisdom filled with experiences of trying to embody the gospel communally. Although none of the communities and experiences represented are the same, we hope that the reader may find in these pages descriptions of a way of life shaped by the same Holy Spirit.

These essays are an attempt to show how some Christians in the church in the United States feel the Spirit leading them to creative ways of life that may provide the hope of new possibilities for faithfulness. In this sense the new monasticism hopes to spark ecumenical conversation in churches across the country about how we should live together as the pilgrim people of God sojourning in a place and time where the powers of darkness still struggle to maintain their fading dominion. At best, we hope these essays will bear fruit that looks like dialog among Christians who share a desire to follow the leading of the Spirit into the joyful hope of life in the kingdom of God, however that may look in diverse local contexts.

We also hope these essays will encourage and challenge

Christian communities to share with one another glimpses of God's reign in order to help us imagine the possibility of participating in Christ's redemptive work in our midst. We know the Spirit works in various and mysterious ways and hope these essays give a taste of how God is delivering us from the powers of darkness. Not all locations are the same, but hopefully these stories of experiments in faithfulness will provoke other communities to search for glimmers of hope breaking through the delusive false-reality of the prince of this world.

Since we need to learn from one another how God is working, we think it is important to share with each other how we see the Spirit moving in our midst. To that end we have launched a website, *www.newmonasticism.org*, to provide a space for continuing the discernment of what a new monasticism might look like. (One of the powers we resist, of course, is technology; so we do this with doubts.) Check the site for upcoming meetings around the country to meet one another face to face.

We live in troubling times, stumbling over ourselves as we discover that the troubles are within and without. So it is with humble hope that we sing, "O Come, O Come Emmanuel" with our friends at Chapel Hill Mennonite Fellowship, who journey with us as we look forward to that heavenly homeland. And thanks to Valparaiso Practice Project who funded this writing, and the good folks at Wipf & Stock who want to publish a book that won't make any money because they think it might possibly serve the church.

Durham, NC
Advent, 2004

12 Marks of a New Monasticism

Moved by God's Spirit in this time called America to assemble at St. John's Baptist Church in Durham, NC, we wish to acknowledge a movement of radical rebirth, grounded in God's love and drawing on the rich tradition of Christian practices that have long formed disciples in the simple Way of Christ. This contemporary school for conversion, which we have called a "new monasticism," is producing a grassroots ecumenism and a prophetic witness within the North American church which is diverse in form, but characterized by the following marks:

1) Relocation to the abandoned places of Empire.

2) Sharing economic resources with fellow community members and the needy among us.

3) Hospitality to the stranger.

4) Lament for racial divisions within the church and our communities combined with the active pursuit of a just reconciliation.

5) Humble submission to Christ's body, the church.

6) Intentional formation in the way of Christ and the rule of the community along the lines of the old novitiate.

7) Nurturing common life among members of intentional community.

8) Support for celibate singles alongside monogamous married couples and their children.

9) Geographical proximity to community members who share a common rule of life.

10) Care for the plot of God's earth given to us along with support of our local economies.

11) Peacemaking in the midst of violence and conflict resolution within communities along the lines of Matthew 18.

12) Commitment to a disciplined contemplative life.

May God give us grace by the power of the Holy Spirit to discern rules for living that will help us embody these marks in our local contexts as signs of Christ's kingdom for the sake of God's world.

www.newmonasticism.org

Introduction

Jonathan R. Wilson

The faithfulness of life embodied in a new monasticism is even more important now than it was when I suggested it in the last chapter of *Living Faithfully in a Fragmented World: Lessons for the Church from MacIntyre's 'After Virtue'*. At that time the chapter on "The New Monasticism" was a thought experiment. I had been convinced, along with many others, that MacIntyre's study in moral theory provided a seminal analysis of our cultural moment. Although Alasdair MacIntyre's own journey had not yet brought him back to the church (a subsequent development that is reflected in his later work), many of us were convinced that his analysis was of profound importance for the church. So I began to draw lessons from *After Virtue* for the life and witness of the church. Most of the lessons were easily recognizable in an academic context—the fragmentation of culture, the failure of the Enlightenment project, the pivotal moment: Nietzsche or Aristotle, the recovery of tradition. These were recognizable once the profound and erudite analysis of MacIntyre was performed.

But what was less recognizable was MacIntyre's final comment, which I describe in *Living Faithfully* (p. 68) as "a clear-eyed pessimism and an enigmatic hope." Drawing a loose parallel between our time and an earlier time, MacIntyre writes:

✳ If my account of our moral condition is correct, we ought also to conclude that for some time now we too have reached that turning point. What matters at this stage is the construction of local forms of community within which civility and the intellectual and moral life can be sustained through the new dark ages which are already upon us. And if the tradition of the virtues was able to survive the horrors of the last dark ages, we are not entirely without grounds for hope. This time, however, the barbarians are not waiting beyond the frontiers; they have already been among us for quite some time. And it is our lack of consciousness of this that constitutes part of our predicament. We are waiting not for Godot, but for another—doubtless very different—St. Benedict.[1]   ✳

When I began to explore this cryptic passage, I realized that the longing for another St. Benedict, when located at the conclusion of MacIntyre's account, followed inexorably from his analysis and identified the essential next step—the formation of a new monasticism.

✱When this longing instructs the church, the local forms of community for which MacIntyre calls are no longer primarily for the sustenance of intellectual and moral life. Nor are they communities that withdraw from the world to insure their own survival and the flourishing of their members. Rather, within the life of the church a new monasticism exists to sustain knowledge of the gospel of the kingdom that was proclaimed, embodied, and accomplished in Jesus Christ. And the communities of the new monasticism exist for the sake of witness to Jesus Christ who is the life and hope of the world.

This volume and the communities represented in its pages is a sign that some are conscious of our predicament. As these communities and the community of communities grows, and as schools

---

[1] Alasdair MacIntyre, *After Virtue: A Study in Moral Theory* (Notre Dame: University of Notre Dame Press, 1984), p.263.

2

for conversion arise from the recognition that the new dark ages are upon us, certain convictions must be maintained to guide the new monasticism in faithful witness.

The New Monasticism is Historically-Situated

Monastic communities have been a persistent feature of the life of the church. They have arisen in different eras in response to a variety of cultural markers. These communities have a family resemblance to one another but they are also shaped by strategic and tactical responses to their particular historical situations. For example, if we think of the Confessing Church seminary that was guided by Dietrich Bonhoeffer as a monastic community in its historical setting, we can understand why it was located in Finkenwalde and not Berlin. Likewise, if we think of the historical setting for the contemporary Sojourners community, we can understand why they relocated from Chicago to Washington, D.C. In Bonhoeffer's setting, in the midst of Nazi Germany, his seminary had to be outside the gaze of the authorities in order for it to fulfill its *telos*. In the same way—in different historical circumstances—the Sojourners community had to move *to* the center of power in order to fulfill its *telos*. These two "monastic" communities acted with equal faithfulness by discerning their historical circumstances and acting in what appear to be opposite ways.

Today's new monasticism (NM) must be historically-situated in the narrative provided by MacIntyre's *After Virtue* and the subsequent rise of a new Empire. Thus, the NM must constantly think through the form of its life and the direction of its mission in light of our cultural history, the fragmentation of our life, the failure of the Enlightenment project, the Nietzschean temptation, and the continual "recovery" of its life as rooted in the good news that God is redeeming creation in, through, and for Jesus Christ.

In light of our cultural history, the NM must live with the social memory (true or not) that the church once ruled Western culture. The NM is not a means of constricting the sphere of Christian influence so that we may maintain a semblance of that cultural dominance on a smaller scale. Rather, the NM is a means of learning and living out the conviction that God is indeed the redeemer of all creation not by imposition but by invitation to enter into the fullness of life as God intends and makes possible through Christ.

In light of the fragmentation of our lives, the NM is a form of life that heals our brokenness by liberating us from "the powers of this dark age" (Eph.5) and providing a place to practice the way of Christ. Since those who form the NM have also been formed by the fragmentation of contemporary life, this means that the task of forming communities of the NM will be marked by deep struggle, perhaps a great deal of pain, and the hard work of reconciliation. The power of Christ's cross as the climactic work of atonement will stand at the center of the NM. In this work of atonement, it is absolutely vital that the NM recognizes and properly names the fragmentation that inhibits and distorts the formation of community and the healing of persons in community. Without this knowledge and the practices of reconciliation, the work of forming a NM can be too painful and too difficult to continue.

In the ruins of the Enlightenment project, the NM must witness in its own life to another path to peace—a path guided not by a putatively ahistorical and universal reason that eradicates all difference in a doomed quest for peace. Rather, the NM will live out a witness to peace rooted in the way of Jesus, a path that celebrates the difference of the Spirit among us that also reconciles us to God and one another in Christ. Thus, the NM makes the practices of peacemaking central to its life together not as a new strategy for accomplishing the Enlightenment project but as a means of witnessing to the work of God in Christ through the presence of the Holy Spirit.

In light of the Nietzschean temptation to accept power over the other as the ultimate reality and guide to life, the NM must continually relearn how true power manifests itself. The easy response to the Nietzschean temptation is the renunciation of power, but that is a response as impossible as it is irresponsible. The power of God's love manifest in Christ and made present in the Holy Spirit is necessary to the formation of disciples of Jesus into new monastic communities. Power *is* present and available in the Spirit; to renounce it is to turn away from the Spirit's presence and work. So the NM displays a reconception of power that witnesses to the self-giving power of Jesus Christ. Here power will be learned as the gift of love in Christ that brings about the flourishing of humankind along with the rest of creation in anticipation of the consummation of that work in a new heavens and a new earth.

The New Monasticism is Eschatologically Directed

At the same time that the NM is historically situated, its response must be directed by its *telos*—the end goal toward which it is headed. Since one of the marks of our cultural moment is the loss of any sense of *telos* and the consequent reduction of all action to the battle for power over the other, the recovery of teleological thinking and living is one, perhaps *the*, critical task of the day. For the NM this teleology must be further specified by *eschatology*—our understanding of the end of history in Jesus Christ. In the Aristotelian tradition from which MacIntyre wrote *After Virtue*, teleology is a highly developed conviction that is interdependent with other convictions, such as Aristotle's metaphysics of biology. That interdependence has led some to question the possibility of recovering teleology in any significant way today. Such questioning may be quite telling when it is directed toward Aristotelian and other earlier teleologies. But for Christians those questions and criticisms are irrelevant, because Christian eschatology replaces teleology as the end or goal toward which any thing and all things are directed. After briefly exploring the significance of eschatology, we can return to the direction that it provides for the NM.

To think eschatologically, Christians must recognize that the end of things cannot simply be inferred from their existence or their nature. That is, thinking eschatologically makes us realize that God's actions are required for the goal or purpose of things to be realized. Living eschatologically, then, means that we must not line our living up with "the way things are" in this age. The way of discipleship to Jesus Christ is not the best strategy for "making life work" or "getting along in this world" as those phrases would be commonly understood. Rather, the way of Jesus is living by that which is seen by the eyes of faith and sustained by the presence of hope; living eschatologically is making present that which is yet to come.

To think and live eschatologically, followers of the way must also recognize that the *telos* of all things embraces both the material and the historical without denying the difference in these two and without erasing one to accomplish the fulfillment of the other. Indeed, for Christians the only way for either to be fulfilled is for both to be fulfilled. In other words, God works in and through history for the redemption of creation, and God brings history to its fulfillment in a new creation.

When we turn to the eschatologically-directed life of the NM, an important point emerges: in the midst of its historical situation and the formation of its life together, the NM *must* cling to this eschatological *telos* if it is to remain true to that which calls it into existence and gives it its mission. The NM must always be oriented toward this *telos* in the midst of many other temptations. Perhaps the greatest temptation faced by the NM is simply the perpetuation of its own life. As a community of the NM struggles through the many challenges of the historical situation that I described above and comes to a place where its life seems to be reflecting its *telos*, the community itself can easily become the reason for the existence of the community. That is, having paid a high price (it seems) for the blessing and peace that marks the community, the protection of all that has been gained can become the new (and false) *telos* of the community. If the life of the community is truly found in its always living toward the eschaton, then it is that future and not the community itself that is the life of the community.

The other great temptation in the life of the NM is to swing from the danger of perpetuating its own life to the equally mistaken conviction that the NM exists for the sake of the world. This seems, at first, to be just the protection against the danger that I identified in the previous paragraph. That is, we could easily fall into the subtle error of concluding that the NM can prevent itself from falling into the error of institutional maintenance by always directing its life toward the world.

This strategy of serving the world to avoid institutional maintenance is *almost* right in its approach, but like the focus on self-preservation, the focus on world-service commits the error of submitting to the penultimate rather than the ultimate. To be eschatologically directed, the NM must orient its life in accordance with the consummation of the kingdom of God—the redemption of creation in Jesus Christ. When this *telos* is honored, then the communities of the NM are sustained not by their own power but by their participation in the coming kingdom. At the same time, the NM that is oriented toward the redemption of creation in Jesus Christ serves the world in proper proportion as the world is being redeemed. The NM serves the world not by focusing on the world but by orienting its life to the kingdom, which is the redemption of the world. The NM serves itself not by concentrating on its own survival but by devoting its life to the eschaton revealed, established and consummated by Jesus Christ.

The New Monasticism is Grace Dependent

Given the historical situation that calls for a NM and the teleological direction of NM (even when transformed by eschatology), perhaps the most difficult direction for the NM is to recognize and live out its dependence upon God's grace. No matter how thoughtful, how committed, how sacrificial, how well-meaning, how self-critical (and the list could go on indefinitely)—no matter how much care communities of the NM devote to remaining faithful, the one thing that makes their life and mission possible is the grace of God.

This grace is not an abstract unreality or an empty slogan. It can be specified even though it cannot be understood or controlled. Grace is the power of God that comes as sheer gift. In the midst of a lively debate about whether a gift can be given, the NM can exist by grace not because the debate has been settled but because the communities of the NM already know the gift of grace.

In the NM dependence upon God's grace comes in very specific ways. That grace is the power that enables the faithful living out of the vision described throughout this book. Grace brings healing and integrity to our fragmented lives. It rebuilds community when our fragmentation threatens to tear us apart. It makes peace among us in our continuing difference. It turns power from self-seeking to kingdom-seeking. It makes us participants in the kingdom that is coming.

For followers in the NM, submitting to our dependence upon grace is vital. Of course, such submission simply is life in Christ. But for the NM, submission to grace is a very specific challenge. Because the NM responds to a particular reading of our historical situation and commits itself to living eschatologically, it is especially susceptible to the temptation of heroism. In her wonderful retrieval of wise monastic theology, Roberta Bondi writes that

> it was an enormous temptation to the beginner to see herself or himself as a hero, confronted with heroic-sized tasks to perform in order to reach that goal of love. Unfortunately, being human, and suffering from human frailty, that same beginner would eventually fail; she would pick a fight with a sister, fall asleep during an all night vigil, eat during a fast. Perhaps a male monk might even follow a girl home from the market. Then would come the inevitable, soul-destroying despair.[2]

This despairing failure of the individual can also be the despairing failure of the community unless it is met by a turn to the grace that undergirds the life of the community and its members.

In order to continually receive this grace, communities of the NM must submit themselves to the same "disciplines of grace" that marks the older monastic communities. The simple task of providing for daily sustenance of life through farming, cooking,

---

[2] Roberta Bondi, *To Love as God Loves* (Philadelphia: Fortress Press, 1987), p.46.

cleaning, and other tasks, reminds us of our dependence. The tasks of praying, worshiping, fasting, and discerning together also open the community to God's grace, though of course they can also be distorted into acts of heroism. Continual openness to others through the central practice of hospitality makes clear the community's dependence upon grace. Finally, the monastic vows of poverty, chastity, and obedience, whatever form they take in the discernment of new monastic communities, are best understood as commitment to a way of life made possible only by God's sustaining and redeeming grace.

The testimony of many forerunners and contemporary communities of NM is that many began with a heroic vision of themselves and their calling. That heroic vision eventually collapses into the illusion that it is. At that point, the community is either rebuilt by God's grace into a true monastic community or it trims its vision and its calling to fit what is possible by human effort. In the latter case, it ceases to witness faithfully to the coming kingdom except insofar as God's judgment comes upon it.

Conclusion

The *Rule of St. Benedict* provided wise guidance for communities of Christ's disciples that contributed to the preservation and propagation of the gospel in previous perilous times. Today in North America and the larger sphere of Western European culture, faithfulness to the gospel is in danger. As our culture's project desperately works to maintain control despite its looming death, the "living arrangement" worked out by the church and the culture is collapsing. Many parts of the church are sinking with the culture and doing so without any resistance. The call for a NM is the work of God's Spirit calling us to renewed understanding of the gospel and faithful witness to it through new forms of monastic community. This chapter seeks to provide strategic guidance as this vision is developed in the following chapters. May God grant us an understanding of our situation, direction toward the eschaton, and grace for our journey.

Mark 1: Relocation to Abandoned Places of Empire

Sr. Margaret M. McKenna

I. *The Deserts I Have Known*

Some time ago, I made the first of three sojourns in Israel. I had been teaching Scripture for some ten years, and had the opportunity to study for three years in Jerusalem and attend *L'Ecole Biblique et Archaeologique Francaise*. For a long time I had had a strong desire to go to Jerusalem, the City of Peace. What better place to update my scripture scholarship? My first year there, I studied Hebrew, French, and German and did some archaeological work at Tel Gerazim. The next two years I was a full time student at the French School of Bible and Archaeology. I lived in a small roof-top apartment with a great view of the Old City and the Judean desert stretching out beyond the Mount of Olives.

For some twenty years I had been busy nurturing community life for newcomers in my Medical Mission Sisters. On the Turkish boat bringing me from Naples to Haifa, I was aware of a longing to experiment with solitude, to experience the desert and live alone. To this end, I made of my apartment a school for the good uses of solitude. And one day a month I boarded an Arab bus to Jericho and got off somewhere in the middle of the Judean desert. I hiked, often along the Wadi Qelt or an old Roman road, first through the steppe land, then through the desert proper, at last through the "chalk hills" that led to Jericho. These whipped cream hills became a symphony of color under the brush of the setting sun. These were wonderful days. I never felt fear. The desert felt friendly to me and taught me trust. I exulted in freedom. No one to please but God alone. The beauty of the flowers and green growth wherever water escaped its open aquaduct, made my heart sing and my body feel light. I fell in love with the desert. My spirit sang with exultation in its silence, grandeur, and intimacy. Nothing and no one but God and God's artistry, it was easy to keep and follow a strong focus that was both inner and outer. Everything was alive and one: God, me, the beautiful sky and contoured earth and all its surprises, vistas, valleys, caves, a spring here, a gorgeous asphodel plant there. Bedouin shepherds and goats tumbled down the side of the hill and over the boulders. A Greek monastery hung on the wadi's cliff. God seemed everywhere, in everything filling the vast space. On one of these desert days in spring, I counted 23 different species of wild flowers, some of them familiar to us, like iris and daisies—all of them in bloom, but no more than an inch or so high. Life seeds were abundant, but water was scarce. Where water was abundant, the flowers were, too; and they and life itself were "supersized."

II. History and Theology of Relocation

I went to the desert to find out what drew Moses, Elijah, Jesus, John the Baptist, the Ammas and the Abbas, Anthony, Syncletica, Pachomius, Barsanuph, Isaac the Syrian, Benedict and Basil, and countless other prophets and saints. What allure does the desert have for God-seekers and lovers of every age? For Hosea? For the couple in the Song of Songs? "What did you go out in the desert to see?" (Lk.7:24), Jesus asks us who want to follow Him today in a world that is falling apart.

The desert lacks many things but offers the opportunity to know God and ourselves. *"Meminisse sui, meminisse Dei."* To be mindful of God is to be mindful of self, as St. Augustine remarked. Because it is empty of distractions and the opportunity to impress others, the desert teaches us the One only and alone is truly necessary. And if we have that focus, we have everything. The wilderness asks us how much we can give up and do without. But its great gift is the solitude that invites us to be ourselves. The chance to be alone before God. Solitude and emptiness are our greatest fears. In the desert we embrace them with complete trust and find God. And in finding God we find ourselves. This is the pearl of great price, surprising Joy!

I swear Isaiah wrote his 35th chapter in the desert of Judah, to give voice to my desert experience.

> The desert and parched land will exult.
>   The steppe will rejoice and bloom
> They will bloom with abundant flowers
> And rejoice with joyful song.
> The glory of Lebanon will be given them
> The splendor of Carmel and Sharon:
> They will see the glory of the Lord
> The splendor of our God…
> Say to those whose hearts are frightened:
>   Be strong, fear not!
> Here is your God…
> Then will the eyes of the blind be opened,
> The ears of the deaf be cleared;
> Then the lame will leap
> And the tongue of the dumb sing.
>
> Streams will burst forth in the desert,
> And rivers in the steppelands…
> No lion will be there
> Nor beast of prey be met there.
> It is for those with a journey to make
> And on it the redeemed will walk.
> They will enter Zion singing,
> Crowned with everlasting joy.
> Sorrow and mourning will flee.

And I can understand why Hosea wanted to make his harlot wife "like a desert," "reduce her to an arid desert and slay her with thirst" in the process of bringing her back to herself and him and God (Hosea 2:5-7). We go to the desert to become again like the desert, natural, empty, true, and capable of being renewed by love. We do the same thing in New Jerusalem, the recovery community where I now live, when we require our newcomers to discontinue all communication with their former contexts for their first sixty days with us. We call this period "blackout" and it is the key to lasting recovery. Actually it is a desert experience, a free fall into an abyss of love.

> So I will allure her;
> I will lead her into the desert
> And speak to her heart.
> I will give her again the vineyards she had.
> And the valley of Achor as a door of hope.
> She will respond there as in the days of her youth.

> ...I will espouse you to me forever:
> I will espouse you in justice, love, mercy and fidelity.
> And you shall know the Lord.
> (Hosea.2:21,22)

The couple in the Song of Songs, be they Solomon and one of his many brides, Israel and/or the church and God, or just two human lovers, are both marked by desert experience. Both are shepherds in the desert. The bride says she is "dark – but lovely... as the tents of Kedar, as the curtains of Salma." Kedar is a Syrian desert region whose name suggests blackness. And tents were often made of black goat skins. The curtains are tent coverings of a region close to Kedar. "Do not stare at me because I am swarthy, because the sun has burned me" (SS 1:3,6). She in turn asks him to tell her where he pastures his flock. He tells her in answer to "Follow the tracks of the flock. And pasture the young ones near the shepherds' camps" (1:7). She is in the city looking desperately for him, when he "comes up from the desert" (3:6). Toward the end of the poem, she also is "coming up from the desert, leaning upon her lover" (5:6).

We hope our blackouts will experience a little of what the prophet Elijah did on Mount Carmel under the broom tree, depressed to the point of praying to die. He received some heavenly food: bread from a raven and water from the stream, in the wadi Cherith, and walked in its strength for forty days and nights to the mountain of God, Horeb, in the desert. There he lived in a cave seeking "to save his life" (I Kgs. 19). And there he found God not in the wind, or earthquake, or fire, but in the sound of silence that asked his heart a question: "Elijah, why are you here?" His answer was basically, "to save my skin!" Then God laid out the shape of his program: "Go outside and stand on the mountain. The Lord will be passing by." Then, "Go. Take the road back to the desert near Damascus." Learn to live with yourself and God alone, and all manner of things will be well.

The desert is the place where the prophets of Israel were transformed by awareness of God's presence and Word and were sent out to proclaim it to the world. It is the place where God's covenant forged the community of Israel, and where His Shekinah presence led them and taught them to trust. It was through a journey through the desert that they returned to Jerusalem from exile and recovered. It is the place where John the Baptist, believed by some to be Elijah *redevivus*, prepared the "Way of the Lord" and baptized Christ.

After his baptism, Jesus went alone into the desert to pray and fast for forty days in the rugged rocks and isolated terrain of the Judean desert. This event is recounted by Matthew (4:1-11), Mark (1:12-13), and Luke (4:1-11). During this time he experienced temptations not unlike the ones that Israel experienced during their forty years in the desert. Satan tried to seduce him with promises of material prosperity, earthly empire and spiritual showmanship, if he would only disobey God and worship him. We see in Jesus a man forced to look at himself and his capacity to misdirect his potential. Jesus experienced our emptiness, uncertainty and vulnerability. All alone with his demon, like Job, Jesus stood in faithfulness to his God. He proved steadfast in trust and obedience to God alone, and quoted Psalm 91 to this effect.

Subsequently, Jesus retreated periodically to lonely and abandoned places to find refreshment and strength in intimacy with God, and invited his disciples to do the same. In the garden and on the cross, he experienced the deceptive feeling of abandonment which is the shadow side of desert experience and the "dark night of the soul" that comes before the dawn of the promised New Day experienced by everyone called to seek God alone.

What is there about relocation that makes it a mark of the new monasticism? Relocation expresses conversion and commitment, the decision to resist imperial pressures and the pleasures and rewards of conformity to the way of all empires: pride, power, and reduction of all values to the "bottom line." It is a coming out from under, a liberation and a real challenge. It is a no-saying and a yes-saying: No to an old way of life and Yes to the search for a new one. It makes it easy and almost necessary to live the Jesus way. It cuts the umbilical cord in birthing Christ-Life and the beloved community. It gives up on patching the pot thrown off balance on the whirling wheel, re-kneads and throws again the clay, centers it carefully this time, and realizes afresh the reworked clay's potential for beauty and service. In a new place one must begin by looking and listening, and this leads to love, creativity, service, and surprise. A new place, inclusive of a new and different environment, blows the mind preoccupied with survival and opens new vistas and a new focus.

And what is the significance for the new monasticism of "abandoned places"? One of Webster's definitions of "desert" is "an abandoned place." An abandoned place is one that has no attraction for the "world of what's happening now," and therefore is left alone by the political, economic, and social powers that be. Deserts and wastelands are abandoned places. So are inner cities, some of the loneliest places on earth. The attraction of the desert is its naturalness, openness and unconventional beauty. It is like a blank canvas to an artist. The blank canvas or wall mirrors an interior state as well as an exterior environment. The blankness is an invitation to renewed spiritual and environmental creativity and transformation. It is also a refuge from the filled and arranged and familiar canvas that society provides.

The post-Constantinian Christians living in the urban Roman Empire found themselves suddenly part of the "dirty, rotten system" of Empire. They were part of a picture that made them sad. The church, their "Beloved Community," was increasingly filled with "joiners." The powerful love of Christ that produced so many martyrs was supplanted by the love of social advantage. Integrity of the few was replaced by the compromises for the many. The peace of Christ evaporated in the military culture required for the maintenance of an empire. The simplicity of the church of the catacombs yielded to the ornate impressiveness that was the signature of imperial art and architecture. Where could they go where there was space for an alternative expression of the Spirit within them in all its freshness and originality? Where was the "Holy Roman Empire" and its military NOT in control? Where were they NOT building churches in the model of empirical halls funded by taxes? They found the answers to their questions in the deserts that surrounded the Mediterranean, in Syria, the Judean desert and in Egypt. These deserts were the refuge of wild beasts and society's outcasts. They were considered dangerous places. But the early faith was that Christ's love can transform any desert and make it a new Eden or a New Jerusalem. So the hardiest Christians, inspired by the spirit of the martyrs and the early church, and longing to experience the original freshness and power of the Spirit, relocated to these harsh but beautiful deserts.

Since then Christians have developed a rich tradition of conscientious relocation to deserts and earth's more secluded corners. Some examples are the early Desert Mothers and Fathers, and the *poustinias* of Russia's forests and deserts. The God-seeking wandering monks and itinerants created an abandoned place by constant wandering. Missionaries left all including home to find God in peoples and places different from their own. There are

contemplatives who create an artificial desert by cloister and en-
closure. The Catholic Workers build "a new society in the shell of
the old," and witness to the "anarchical personalism" of the nonviolent and unconventional Jesus. The followers of Charles de
Foucault create their desert in the impersonal and poorly-paid
workplaces of the modern world as well as in deserts. Addicts of
our times offer another expression of the potential of transformative relocation by leaving the violent and destructive culture of the
streets to seek a new way of life in recovery communities. Peace
activists of our time have embraced the desert experience in prison
cells as Peter and Paul, Gandhi and Martin Luther King did before
them, and witnessed its hidden richness in their writings.

But, since literal desert experiences are the incarnation of the
metaphorical image of the desert in the spiritual journey, it is
most valuable perhaps for us to accent them. So, we will focus on
the classic desert experience of the Abbas and Ammas of the
fourth century in the deserts of Egypt, Syria, and Palestine. These
were people who, as Merton puts it, "swam for their life"[1] against
the disastrous currents of their civilized context on the way to
shipwreck. In the words of Basil Pennington in his preface to
Desert Fathers, "they fled an increasingly worldly Church to the
freedom of the desert."[2] They were not behind, but perhaps ahead
of their time, and even of ours. They were anarchists of sorts,
Merton remarks, who did not let themselves be passively led by a
decadent state, but wanted to find a way their inner Spirit could
be free and express itself afresh. Their idea was not to place
themselves above society, not to fly from human companionship
but to give expression to the reign of God, rather than conform to
the society that oppressed them. What they sought most of all
was their own true self, in Christ. "They sought a God whom they
alone could find, not one who was given," Merton writes, a God
of their understanding, not of anybody else's. They conformed

---

[1] Thomas Merton, *The Wisdom of the Desert* (New York City: New Directions,
1970).
[2] Helen Wadell, *The Desert Fathers* (New York: Random House, 1998), Preface,
p. xvi.

only to the will of God as they understood it with the help of scripture and those more experienced than they. Hence Abbot Anthony's advice: "Therefore, whatever you see your soul to desire according to God, do that thing, and you shall keep your heart safe." The hermits sought to die to transient existence as Christ died on the cross, and rise with Him in the light of a "new wisdom." This involved "struggle," the goal of which was "purity of heart" or simplicity, the great early Christian ideal of *haplotes*—"the single eye"—an intuitive vision of one's reality as lost and found in God. This awareness brought rest. "At peace in the possession of a sublime 'Nothing' the spirit laid hold, in secret, upon the 'All'—without trying to know what it possessed." These hermits then, Merton tells us, "made a clean break" with a conventional, accepted social context in order to "swim for their lives into an apparent void." That void was the wellspring of their originality, and the precious freshness of their recorded sayings.

We know the early hermits from their "sayings," *Verba Seniorum* in Migne's *Latin Patrology* (Vol. 73). The *Lives of the Fathers* lack this primitive freshness and originality by comparison. The *Verba* are always simple and human, and full of common-sense, never abstract. They come from simple and silent people, unselfconscious about what they had to say. It is the later fables about their ascetic feats that gave them the reputation of fanaticism.

Most of the stories concern hermits of Nitria and Scete in Northen Egypt. The Thebaid, near ancient Thebes, was another center of monastic life. Palestine attracted monks and hermits from all over the then known world, including Sts. Jerome, Paula and Eustochia who translated scripture in a cave at Bethlehem. The book of Barsanuph's Correspondence with John of Gaza (*La Correspondence de Barsanuph et Jean de Gaza*, a French translation of the original Syriac) is the only, and very engaging, firsthand account we have of the spiritual mentorship of a desert father by an elder (senex or abba, the terms are synonymous). Barsanuph protected his solitude by asking disciples to write their questions, and he wrote his answers. Copies of these were collected by his novice-secretary.

Novices usually lived with a Senior Abba or Amma. The Seniors lived on their own but sought advice from those more experienced. At certain times all the solitaries and novices would come together for the liturgical *synaxis*. The latter sometimes included a common meal and a meeting. In solitude, they worked and prayed. The ideal was to "pray always." Constant repetition, conscious and subconscious, of the prayer of the Publican—"Jesus, Son of God, Saviour, have mercy on me"—was one way to achieve it. The hermit was supposed to be peaceful and stay as much as possible in one place. Mobility was to be downward, not upward; inner, not outer.

They supported themselves by the work of their hands such as basket-weaving and gardening. Products were sold in nearby towns. Hospitality was top priority, and took preference over fasting. They were the very opposite of misanthropes. According to Cassian's *Monastic Institutions* there was more real love in the desert than in the cities. The primacy of love as spiritual identification with others, over everything else that comprised desert life, is evident in the "Sayings." An immense reverence characterized their interactions.

And there is no minimization of the difficulties involved or of the lengths their love would go. For example, Abbot Ammonas spent fourteen years praying to be delivered from anger. Abbot Serapion sold his last book, a copy of the Gospels, and gave the money to the poor. Self is the price of love. The great and gentle Abbot Moses, often called "Black Moses," refused to join in a communal reproof of a delinquent by walking into the severe assembly with a basket of sand and letting the sand run out through many holes. "My own sins are running out like this sand," he said, "and yet I come to judge the sins of another." Then there were the two old brothers who had lived together for years without a quarrel, who decided to "get into an argument like the rest of men," but simply could not succeed.

Saint Anthony, though not the first hermit, became the most influential through the biography of him written by St. Athanasius.[3]

---

[3] A contemporary translation of "The Life of Antony" is available in the Classics of Western Spirituality Series from Paulist Press (tr. Robert C. Gregg).

This writing created a great stir in the Roman world. Desert vocations multiplied so much that as the title of a book by D.J. Chitty says, "the desert became a city." The popular impression is that Anthony was something of a spiritual Superman, enjoying his combats with the devil. But in fact he was a free-spirited, well-balanced, sensible and attractive human being. He counsels that we are only vulnerable in our diabolic encounters to the degree that we are afraid and lacking in confidence in God.

The Ammas are predictably less quoted than the Abbas, but Amma Syncletica (ca. 400 AD) has some wisdom to offer on our topic of abandoned places.

> Not all courses are suitable for all people. You should have confidence in your own disposition. For many it is profitable to live in community; for others it is helpful to withdraw on their own.... Many people have found salvation in a city while imagining the conditions of a desert. And many, though on a mountain, have been lost by living the life of townspeople. It is possible for one who is in a group to be alone in thought, and for one who is alone to live mentally with a crowd. (*Life of Syncletica*)

> We have committed ourselves to exile, that is, we are outside secular boundaries; we have, then, been banished – let us not seek the same ends. (*Life of Syncletica*).

The "Life of St. Pelagia the Harlot" by James the Deacon, and the "Life of Saint Mary the Harlot" by St. Ephraim of Edessa are other wonderful sources that illustrate the Lives of the Ammas.[4]

III. Some New Expressions of Relocation to Abandoned Places of Empire

So what new forms could the classical desert take in the world

---

[4] For more on these sources see Hugh Feiss, *Monastic Wisdom*.

of the twenty-first-century? The possibilities are endless. Catholic Worker Houses, the Simple Way, The Open Door, New Jerusalem, The Bruderhof, Jonah House, Camden House, Rutba House, and countless others illustrate the endless possibilities. The following desert-inspired ingredients seem to influence their development: God-seeking and prayer will have the primary place, but be thoroughly integrated with life and witness. We will build the practice of Sabbath freedom into the rhythms of our calendars, lives and work. Our reverence and love for God will be connected to and include all of God's creation. Hospitality in the form of sharing food, roof and friendship with neighbors will foster both compassion and engagement and will be a form of holy communion with marginal cultures and poor populations. The issues of our time, such as militarism, nuclearism, poverty, homelessness, and ecological problems, as manifested on the margins, will call for our personal and communal conversion in the form of disciplined resistance in lifestyle and engagement in the search for solutions. This resistance and engagement will be as much prayer as it is work. Promotion of alternatives to violence and imprisonment will be practiced as well as promoted. Presence and witness will have a prophetic quality that comes from God's Spirit. Personalist and communal rather than institutional models of organization will be characteristic. Numbers and finance will not dominate or dictate our concerns. We will not allow ourselves to be intimidated by the "Powers" of Empire. We will employ the organic (yeast-like), grassroots model that starts with oneself and reaches to ever-widening circles, rather than the top-down approach to social transformation. We will live and witness from the inside out. With the early Christians and the desert hermits of the fourth-century, we will invite the Holy Spirit to reveal possibilities of creative non-participation in Empire's oppressive self-glorification. What we promote, we will begin by practicing. Ordinariness rather than impressiveness will mark the style. The pursuit of a healthy reciprocity of receiving as well as giving will be a practice of humility, respect and justice.

All these practices are expressions of love for all in God. They call us and our world out of injustice and violence, to conversion and wholeness. They inspire the spirit of communion and community that grows out of prayer and a single-eyed focus on God and all in God, whose Spirit is the source of all creativity, integrity, life, and love.

"Relocation to the abandoned places of Empire" is an important mark of the new monasticism. In itself, relocation to abandoned places of Empire is a powerful liturgy of conversion and commitment freely and lovingly undertaken. It is the initiation into the rich and ever-deepening spiritual adventure of the journey into the desert.

I will briefly describe the impact of relocation to abandoned places on a few of the examples mentioned above with which I am most familiar: Catholic Worker Communities, Jonah House, and New Jerusalem Now.

Catholic Worker Houses, founded by Dorothy Day and Peter Maurin, are typically of two kinds: urban or farm. Both exemplify insertion in abandoned places marked by poverty and marginal populations. The practices of hospitality and works of mercy are personalist—that is, direct, personal sharing, rather than institutional. Ideally, urban and farm communities are interrelated, the farms supplying food for the urban soup-kitchens. The practice of the works of mercy, of nonviolence and deep reverence for Christ in the people who come to share community life and hospitality, is the essence of the Catholic Worker life-style and work. They promote peace and justice and practice them vigorously in their lifestyle. They practice what they promote, and their concern for the world is as broad as it is localized. Catholic Workers typically are minimally credentialed by both church and state. They resist taxes and military involvements. They see interest as the evil that makes capitalism the cause of ever increasing suffering for the poor. "The rich get richer and the poor, poorer."

The Catholic Worker Houses witness through nonviolent direct action to their resistance to what Dorothy Day calls "the dirty rotten system" (i.e., the Empire), and often follow her example in their readiness to suffer jail time for their biblically-inspired resistance. Catholic Workers and their communities, although each is unique, all exemplify the traits of the new monasticism. Married couples with children are not infrequently the kernel of new communities, although there are many celibates and singles of all ages. They live in urban deserts where hospitality means sharing in a life of poverty. The pursuit of prayer, the circulation of newsletters, and freedom to experiment, makes these communities spiritually, intellectually and artistically lively and challenging. The original Catholic Worker of NYC, Dorothy Day House and The Olive Branch in D.C., The House of Grace (which provides a free medical clinic) and Philadelphia Catholic Worker in Philadelphia, The Little Flower in Virginia and perhaps fifty others, are old and new examples of the vibrancy of this expression of the spirit of the new monasticism.

Jonah House of Baltimore was founded by Phil and Liz Berrigan, parents of three children, now young adults freely opting to resist the powers of Empire. This family has been the central kernel of the Jonah House community which is closely related to the Catholic Worker Houses in life-style and philosophy, and organizes much nonviolent peace activity together with them. Phil Berrigan, a beloved leader and mentor, died more than a year ago but continues to inspire others to walk in his faithful footsteps. The Jonah House has been a school of seriously committed resistance and faith reflection for many who have lived in it for some years. It has been a source of clear-headed and biblically-based resistance to the most serious evils of our time: first-strike nuclear weaponry, war, oppression, poverty, and ecological disaster, due to the impact of this world's spirit of Empire. It is a house of world-wide love. It has a strong dedication to faith-based resistance and action. Focus and discipline mark its generous spirit.

New Jerusalem Now is a community of mostly African-American, formerly homeless addicts seeking recovery from drugs and alcohol. This community of five houses has been developing in North Central Philadelphia for about twelve years. The "relocation" involved in this community is from life on the streets to a new way of life based on spirituality. What characterizes it is self-help: one addict helping another. It is initially structured in a way that provides help for the less experienced, by those one step ahead of them. One hour daily of Bible study provides a common basis for developing the sought-after "new way of life" which contrasts dramatically with the old one. Love, community, connection with God, strong communal support in behavioral and attitudinal change, are the chief therapies practiced, along with one-on-ones, and "talking about it" in group work. New Jerusalem's pursuit of recovery is in fact a pursuit of fullness of life, love and joy. The philosophy of New Jerusalem is that you cannot fully recover from addiction to drugs and alcohol as an individual, without helping the society that made you sick recover.

Resident members share whatever resources they have with the community and focus their energy on re-organizing their lives on the basis of keeping God first. That re-organization involves as much giving as receiving. The day includes two and one-half hours of "community service," plus daily chores and cooking. Community service includes several forms of food-distribution to the neighborhood, gardening, making murals and beautifying our neighborhood, running workshops on Alternatives to Violence (two three-day workshops every month) for recovering people, neighbors, and court-mandated people. Members do a significant amount of peace and justice work in the form of demonstrations and marches against war and injustice and for human rights, especially economic human rights.

In summary, "relocation to the abandoned places of Empire" is a dynamic force in the developments of communities related to the new monasticism and invites on-going reflection and action. Truly it is the Spirit that leads us there. All the relocations in my own life include:

> joining the Medical Mission Sisters, an international religious community,
> studying and living in Jerusalem and Israel for seven years,
> moving into an African American neighborhood in Germantown,

studying at the University of Pennsylvania and teaching at
La Salle,

joining a French Benedictine contemplative monastery in
Israel,

living as a hermit in the back of the Medical Mission Sisters' barn,

becoming a nonviolent peace activist and spending four
months in jail,

moving to North Philadelphia to start New Jerusalem Laura,

immersion in addiction and recovery,

and the evolution of New Jerusalem Now, a community of
fifty formerly homeless recovering addicts in five self-
run households which express the spirit of the new
monasticism movement...

Every relocation has been a blessing—a source of new challenge
and grace, freeing me from old paradigms and opening me to
pursue the Spirit's movement in my heart, to seek, love and serve
the God I am only beginning to know. I wouldn't have missed a
single step, though some were painful. My journey through all
these twists and turns has had one consistent direction: away
from the distortions in my heart caused by the spirit of Empire,
and towards God and the New Jerusalem, the Beloved Community of Her dreams and ours.

Mark 2: Sharing Economic Resources with Fellow Community Members and the Needy Among Us

Shane Claiborne

I. Downward Mobility in an Upscale World

Following Jesus has been for me a roller-coaster of economic extremes, from serving alongside Mother Teresa amongst the "poorest of the poor" in Calcutta to working at the "mega-church" Willow Creek in the verdant suburbs of Chicago. The footsteps of Jesus seem to lead to rich rulers and poor widows, to villages and cities, to flipping tables and getting dragged before judges. Our community, The Simple Way, was itself born out of the struggle of homeless families needing housing. Beneath the messy collisions of wealth and poverty, I can hear the whisper of a new monasticism.

I was raised in the Bible belt, smothered with Christianity, but thirsty for God. I gorged myself on products within the Christian industrial complex – music, books, even candy "Testa-mints." Economically, we were comfortable—not rich, not poor. But the more I studied Jesus, the more the words of this baby refugee collided with the Christendom surrounding me. In a prominent United Methodist Church I attended there was a stained glass window installed that cost over $100,000. Meanwhile I read John Wesley's words: "If I should die with more than ten pounds, may everyone call me a liar and a thief for I have betrayed the Gospel." Things did not add up. I longed for Jesus to bust out of that stained glass window. I became very disenchanted with the church; yet I was still quite fascinated with Jesus of Galilee. I wondered if there were other restless people asking the question with me: *what if Jesus meant the stuff he said?*

Having helped organize the Bush/Quayle campaign in East Tennessee in 1992, I was not very interested in "liberal" ideas, but I wanted to be with people who were trying to take the Gospel seriously, and I saw very few people doing that regardless of their political leanings. I ended up going to school in Philadelphia, surrounded by people who did not look and think like me. I hoped Jesus would come out of the stained glass window. And He did. But not in the halls of academia.

While studying at Eastern College, I heard about a group of homeless families who had organized themselves and moved into an abandoned cathedral in North Philadelphia. We read in the newspaper that they were facing an eviction from the Archdiocese. The church was kicking homeless people out? Wrestling with God's call to "love your neighbor as yourself," we could not sit still. It was not long before we had piled into a car and headed into a neighborhood we were told never to go near. I remember the first time we went to the cathedral. On the gigantic red doors, the families had hung a banner that read: "How can we worship a homeless man on Sunday and ignore one on Monday." We couldn't.

A powerful student movement emerged on campus, calling ourselves the YACHT Club (Youth Against Complacency and Homelessness Today). We had worship services, took over chapels, preached on cafeteria tables. It was a revival of sorts. In that old cathedral in North Philadelphia, I was reborn. The families became our teachers and theologians. They lived in the wasteland of the corporate economy that I had only read about in sociology class. The Gospel was their language, and they opened our eyes to the economy of the early church. Days, weeks, months passed. Many of the families got housing. Eventually, a group of us from Eastern settled into a rowhouse in Kensington, calling ourselves "The Simple Way" (a tax exempt 501c3 *anti*-profit organization) and trying to discover another way of doing life. Over the years, hundreds of people have come in and out of our life. We continue to dream, and new folks bring new visions. Seven years into it, we find ourselves part of a movement much bigger than The Simple Way—a community of communities that looks to us like a new monasticism.

II. Economics in Scripture and Tradition

Beyond Brokerage

Not long ago, a few friends and I were talking with some very wealthy executives about what it means to be the church and to follow Jesus. One businessman confided, "I, too, have been thinking about following Christ and what that means… so I had this made." He pulled up his shirt-sleeve to reveal a bracelet, engraved with WWJD (*What Would Jesus Do?*). It was custom-made of twenty-four karat gold. Maybe each of us can relate to this man – both his earnest desire to follow Jesus and his distorted execution of that desire, so bound up in the materialism of our culture.

The more I've gotten to know rich folks, the more I am convinced that the great tragedy in the church is not that rich Christians do not care about the poor, but that rich Christians do not *know* the poor. A few years back I surveyed people who said they were "strong followers of Jesus." Over 80 percent agreed with the statement, "Jesus spent much time with the poor." Yet only 1 percent said that they themselves spent time with the poor. Mother Teresa said, "Today it is very fashionable to talk about the poor. Unfortunately it is not as fashionable to talk to the poor." Layers of insulation separate the rich and the poor from truly encountering one another. There are the obvious ones like picket fences and SUVs, and there are the more subtle ones like charity. Tithes, tax-exempt donations, and short-term mission trips, while they accomplish some good, can also function as outlets that allow us to appease our consciences and still retain a safe distance from the poor.

It is much more comfortable to de-personalize the poor so that we do not feel responsible for the catastrophic human failure that someone is on the street while people have spare bedrooms in their homes. We can volunteer in a social program or distribute excess food and clothing through organizations, but rarely do we actually open up our homes, our beds, our dinner tables. When we get to heaven and are separated into sheep and goats, I don't believe Jesus is going to say, "When I was hungry you gave a check to the United Way and they fed me," or, "When I was naked, you donated clothes to the Salvation Army and they clothed me." Jesus is not seeking distant acts of charity. He is seeking concrete actions of love: "you fed me... you visited me, ... you welcomed me in... you clothed me..." (Matt. 25).

When the church becomes a place of brokerage rather than an organic community, she ceases to be alive. Brokerage turns the church into an organization rather than a new family of re-birth. She ceases to be something we are, the living Bride of Christ. The church becomes a distribution center, a place where the poor come to get stuff and the rich come to dump stuff. Both go away satisfied (the rich feel good, the poor get fed), but no one leaves transformed—no new community is formed. People do not get crucified for charity. People are crucified for disrupting the status quo, for calling forth a new world. People are not crucified for helping poor people. People are crucified for joining them.

No doubt, generosity is a biblical value. Generosity is not just a virtue of those with "gifts of mercy." It is at the very heart of our rebirth. Popular culture has taught us to believe that charity is a gift. For Christians it is only what is expected. We have no right not to be charitable. The early Christians taught that charity was merely returning what we have stolen. St. Vincent DePaul said that when he gives bread to the beggars he gets on his knees and asks forgiveness from them.

Economics of Rebirth
I'd like to suggest that, rather than a simple vow of poverty,

we see this mark as a form of simplicity rooted in love. Redistribution is not a prescription for community. Redistribution is a description of what happens when people fall in love with each other across class lines. The author of Acts did not say, "They were of one heart and mind because they sold everything" (Acts 4:32). They held all in common precisely because they were of one heart and mind, as rich and poor found themselves born again into a family where some had extra and others were desperately in need. Redistribution was not systematically regimented but flowed naturally out of a love for God and neighbor. I am not a communist, nor am I a capitalist. As one person put it: "When we truly discover love, capitalism will not be possible and Marxism will not be necessary."

The early Christians said if a child starves while the Christian has extra food, then the Christian is guilty of murder. Basil the Great, writing in the fourth century, put it this way: "When someone strips a man of his clothes we call him a thief. And one who might clothe the naked and does not – should not he be given the same name? The bread in your cupboard belongs to the hungry; the coat in your wardrobe belongs to the naked; the shoes you let rot belong to the barefoot; the money in your vaults belongs to the destitute." Or, in the words of Dorothy Day, "If you have two coats, one of them belongs to the poor." No wonder John the Baptist used to connect redistribution with repentance, as he declared "Repent for the Kingdom of God is at hand... if you have two tunics give one away" (Luke 3:11).

Our simplicity is not an ascetic denunciation of material things to attain personal piety, for "we can sell all that we have and give it to the poor" but if we have not love it is meaningless (1 Cor. 13:3). And there are many progressive liberals who have taught me that we can live lives of disciplined simplicity and still be distant from the poor. We can eat organic, have a common pool of money, and still be enslaved to Mammon. Rather than being bound up by how much stuff we need to buy, we can be enslaved to how simply we must live—thus exchanging one god for another.

Theology of Enough

In addition to rooting simplicity in love, it also seems crucial that our economic practices be theologically grounded. I am convinced that most of the terribly disturbing things which are happening in our world in the name of Christ and Christianity are primarily the result not of malicious people, but of bad theology (at least, I want to believe that). So, rather than distancing ourselves from religious language and biblical study we dive into the Scriptures together, meeting bad theology with good theology, meeting distorted understandings of the warrior God by embodying our allegiance to the slaughtered lamb, meeting the health and wealth Gospel by following the Homeless Rabbi.

How often we hear Christians speak about "believers," concerning themselves only with doctrine, dividing over theological differences, making "orthodoxy" the only criteria for discipleship. Most activism revolves around "orthopraxy"—doing the right things. I believe the power of monasticism is the fusion of these two into a movement that is both theologically grounded and offers practical alternatives to the world's pattern of inequality. Most people know what Christians believe, but if you ask them how Christians live they do not know. We have not shown them. The praxis of the new monasticism is most magnetic when it is grounded in a *theology of enough*.

Essentially, this theology is anchored in the idea that God did not create too many people or not enough stuff. Poverty was not created by God, but by you and me because we have not learned to love our neighbor as ourselves. Gandhi put it well: "There is enough for everyone's need, but there is not enough for everyone's greed." One of the first commands given to our ancestors in the desert (before the Big 10) is: "Each one is to gather only as much as s/he needs" (Exodus 16). God rains down manna from heaven and assures them if they will not take extra there will be enough. When they do take extra, God sends maggots to destroy their stockpile. They are ordered to carry with them one "omer" which was symbolic of their daily providence of bread. Of course, we

31

hear the subtle echoes of this in the Lord's prayer as we are taught to pray for our daily bread—not just *my* bread, but *our* bread. Then we hear the words that Paul reiterates in 2 Corinthians 8:15: "Those who gathered more had no surplus, and those who gathered less had no shortage."

Deuteronomy 15 gives another glimpse of the source of poverty. God goes from saying, "There should be no poor among you," to "If there are poor," to "There will always be poor among you." Even though there is enough, human greed and systemic injustice will always create poor people in the land, so God teaches us personal responsibility to our poor neighbor. God also establishes the Jubilee economy to dismantle the human systems that create poverty– releasing debt, setting slaves free, redistributing property. Folks always say the Israelites never fully lived out the Jubilee. Our friend Ched Myers says, "That's no excuse to ignore God's commands. That's like saying we don't need to worry about the Sermon on the Mount since Christians have never fully practiced it."

There is deep wisdom in the early desert monastic asceticism and the vow of poverty of centuries-old monastic movements, and yet when I talked to my neighbors and homeless friends about a "vow of poverty" they either laughed or gave me a puzzled stare. "Have you ever been poor," some asked. I began to see how myopic my vision and how narrow my language was. It reeked of privilege. So I would suggest we need a third way, neither the prosperity gospel nor the poverty gospel, but the Gospel of abundance rooted in a theology of enough. As Proverbs says: "Give me neither poverty nor riches, but give me only my daily bread. Otherwise, I may have too much and disown you and say, 'Who is the Lord?'" (Proverbs 30:8-9).

Biblical Economics

In the Gospel we see rebirth and redistribution bound up in one another. Of course Jesus' own teaching is packed with stories of debt, workers' wages, redistribution, caring for the poor. His two accounts of the afterlife have unmistakable economic dimensions (the rich man and Lazarus, and the sheep and the goats). We cannot say we love God and pass by our hungry neighbor (James 2:14-17). No one has seen God, but as we love one another God lives with us (1 John 4:12). One of the signs of Pentecost was that there were no needy persons among them, for they shared everything in common (Acts 4:34).

So while the Scriptures are laced full of teaching on economics, for this mark of our new monasticism I want to focus on one passage in particular: Mark 10, particularly verses 29-31: "I tell you the truth, Jesus replied, no one who has left home or brothers or sisters or mother or father or children or fields for me and the Gospel will fail to receive a hundred times as much in this present age (homes, brothers, sisters, mothers, children, and fields – and with them, persecutions) and in the age to come, eternal life. But many who are first will be last, and the last first." In our journey of new monasticism, I think this text gives us one of the clearest glimpses of why redistribution is necessary and to be celebrated.

Immediately preceding this text, Jesus has had his infamous encounter with the rich ruler. After hearing that you must enter the Kingdom like a little kid, a wealthy man comes up and asked Jesus what he needs to do, and Jesus tells him he lacks one little thing: "Sell everything you have and give it to the poor!" The man's face sinks in and he walks away with his riches (v. 21-22).

I think it broke Jesus' heart to let the man walk away. The text says that Jesus looks at him and "loves him" as he walks away (v.21). Jesus doesn't run after him and say, "Hey, it's a journey, just give half," or, "Start with 10%." He simply lets the man choose his wealth. In our culture of "seeker sensitivity" and radical inclusivity, the great temptation is to compromise the cost of discipleship in order to draw a larger crowd. With the most sincere hearts, we do not want to see anyone walk away from Jesus because of the discomfort of his cross, so we pare the claws on the Lion a little—we clean up the passion we are called to follow a bit. I think this is where the disciples were. They protest in awe, "who then can be saved?" (v. 26)—*why must you make it so hard?*

We need some rich folks here, Jesus… we're trying to build a move-ment! And yet Jesus lets him walk away.

Jesus doesn't exclude rich people, he just let's them know it will cost them everything they have. The story is not so much about whether or not rich folks are welcome, but it is about the nature of the Kingdom of God which has an economy diametri-cally opposed to that of the world. Rather than accumulating stuff for oneself, followers of Jesus abandon everything, trusting in God alone for provision. The disciples start to get it saying, "we have left everything" (v.28).

I am excited about eternal life with our Father in heaven. And yet that is not my primary motivation for following Jesus. Even if there were no heaven and there were no hell, I would follow Jesus for the life I have now. Here's the incredible clincher in these verses: the multiplication is not just in the age to come—streets of gold, mansions in heaven, Cadillacs and crowns. The multiplica-tion of resources begins "in this present age." Both the health-and-wealthers and the penitent ascetics miss the deepest reality of these verses which teach us a new economic vision. As we abandon our possessions and biological families, we trust that others too are abandoning their possessions and families, and that there will be an abundance that begins now and lasts for eternity.

III. Some Glimpses of God's New Economy

Mother Teresa: Fasting

People often ask me what Mother Teresa was like. (Some-times it's like they wonder if she glowed in the dark.) She was short, wrinkled, and precious—maybe even a little ornery. But there is one thing I will never forget: her feet. Her feet were deformed. Each morning in mass, I would stare at them. I won-dered if she had contracted leprosy. But I was not going to ask, "Hey, Mother, what's wrong with your feet?" One day a sister asked us, "Have you noticed her feet?" We nodded curiously. Then she continued, "Her feet are deformed because we get just enough donated shoes for everyone, and Mother does not want anyone to get stuck with the worst pair, so she digs through and finds them. Years of doing that have deformed her feet." Years of loving her neighbor as herself deformed her feet.

Perhaps this is the mystery of fasting, as Isaiah tells us. One thing fasting does is sacrifice privilege. Some of us will need to fast to connect us, not only with God, but to our hungry neighbors. Others of us are hungry, and will now be able to dine in the abundance of the Lord's feast. Certainly the 35,000 children starving to death today need not fast to connect to God. But we may need to fast in order to connect to them and to God. No wonder the Corinthian church was scolded for disgracing the Eucharist by allowing some people to come to the table hungry while others are stuffed full. They were not reconciled with one another and needed first to leave the altar and care for their neighbor.

Atom

In our community we have Atom. Atom, as you can tell from his name, is a scientist. He started working on his PhD when he was 21. When Atom encountered Jesus in new ways by living amongst the poor, he was tempted to leave everything, be a bike messenger, and pray all day. (Actually, he did try that for a little while.) But the more he sought God and his gifts, Atom felt his vocation transformed. He was still a scientist, but as he studied science in the context of his global neighborhood, he saw that lack of access to clean water was the biggest killer of children in our world. Over 20,000 kids die each day from water-born, curable diseases. In the year 2025 economists predict the leading cause of violence and war will not be oil, but water. So Atom has dedicated much of his life to studying and working with local indigenous communities to address this crisis. Atom sees that an important part of his service to God's Kingdom is learning to ask the right questions around economics, which are not the same ones as 20 years ago. Many Christian colleges are just now implementing programs like Urban Studies, decades late. Hopefully, Atom and others can convince them to offer tracks on Global Economics before it is too late.

Radical Sharing

Interdependent community also has a way of making the market economy irrelevant. One of our neighbors owns a pizza parlor around the corner. The owner and his family are from Afghanistan, and during the war his loved ones became refugees. He heard about our efforts for peace, bringing attention to the desperate situation in Afghanistan. He made our pizzas with love and joy, sincerely thanking us for what we do. And he always told us to name our own price, for money was irrelevant.

Another family very dear to our hearts owns the Josefina mini-mart across the street from us. Over the years we have become inseparable. The kids come over for homework, participate in our theater camp, and beat us at Skip-Bo (though they cheat sometimes). We helped rehab their house; they helped teach us Spanish. Oftentimes they need transportation to restock the store or pick up the kids. We found that we could insure them (actually at no extra cost) under our policy. So we share cars and resources, and they never take our money for groceries. We are not good Samaritans, nor are we an efficient non-profit provider. We are family with them, and money has lost its relevance. As one of the early Christians said, "Starve mammon with your love." I hope Mammon goes hungry around here.

Practicing Jubilee

A couple of years ago we had two things happen. First, we won a lawsuit for police misconduct in New York City. The police had been arresting homeless people for sleeping in public, and charging them with disorderly conduct. I was arrested one night as I slept out in protest. Through a long legal process, I was found not guilty and filed a civil suit of wrongful arrest, wrongful prosecution, and police misconduct. And we won, in addition to a legal precedent, around $10,000. We knew it did not belong to me or to The Simple Way, but to the homeless in New York for all they endure. It was their victory. The second thing that happened was that after our study of biblical economics, we had an anonymous gift of $10,000 which had been invested in the Stock Market and now was being returned to the poor. A bunch of us started conspiring, and before long we said: "It is time for a celebration of God's Jubilee." And where else should we have it but on Wall Street, in the face of the world's economy? This was not a one-time celebration, but an ancient celebration going back to Leviticus 25 and an eternal celebration of the New Jerusalem. We decided to send 100 dollars to 100 different communities that incarnate the spirit of Jubilee and the economics of love. Each $100 bill had "love" written on it. And we invited everyone to Wall Street for the Jubilee.

After months of laughter and dreaming, it really happened. About 40 people had all the change they could carry—over 30,000 coins in bags, coffee mugs, briefcases, backpacks. Another 50 people would be meeting us on Wall Street. A dozen "secret stashers" ran ahead, hiding hundreds of two-dollar bills all over lower Manhattan in parks, napkin holders, and phone booths. At 8:15 we started trickling into the public square in front of the main entrance to the New York Stock Exchange. Word of the redistribution had spread throughout New York, and nearly 100 folks from the alleys and projects were gathered. We had choreographed the celebration like a play production, making Wall Street the stage of our theatrics of counter-terror. At 8:20, Sister Margaret and I stepped forward to proclaim the Jubilee:

> Some of us have worked on Wall Street and some of us have slept on Wall Street. We are a community of struggle. Some of us are rich people trying to escape our loneliness. Some of us are poor folks trying to escape the cold. Some of us are addicted to drugs and others are addicted to money. We are a broken people who need each other and God, for we have come to recognize the mess that we have created of our world and how deeply we suffer from that mess.
>
> Now we are working together to give birth to a new society within the shell of the old. Another world is possible.

Another world is necessary. Another world is already here. The money for this Jubilee Celebration was formerly invested in the Stock Market. Over $10,000 has been set free, poured out to be shared with our sisters and brothers in need. This money belongs to the poor, the workers, the refugees, the homeless… to all those who have suffered most from the wreckage of the current system. May we return it with joy, with our heads bowed in repentance, and with our hearts lifted in Jubilee.

Then Sister Margaret blew the ram's horn (like our Jewish ancestors used to), and we announced: "Let the celebration begin!" Ten people stationed on balconies above the crowd threw hundreds of dollars in paper money, covering the sky. Then they dropped banners which read, "STOP TERRORISM… SHARE," "love," and "THERE IS ENOUGH FOR EVERYONE'S NEED BUT NOT ENOUGH FOR EVERYONE'S GREED."

The streets turned silver. Our "pedestrians," "tourists," "homeless," and "business people" began pouring out their change. We decorated the place with sidewalk chalk and filled the air with bubbles. Joy was contagious. Someone bought bagels and started giving them out. People started sharing their winter clothes. One of the street-sweepers winked at us as he flashed a dustpan full of money. Another guy hugged someone and said, "Now I can get my prescription filled."

It worked. We had no idea what would happen. We knew it was dangerous, intentionally bringing God and Mammon face to face. But this is precisely what we have committed our lives to. It is risky, and yet we are people of faith, believing that giving is more contagious than hoarding, that love can convert hatred, light can overcome darkness, and grass can pierce concrete— even on Wall Street.

Mark 3: Hospitality to the Stranger

Maria Russell Kenney

I. The Experience of Hospitality: Our Own Story

When he first wandered in the door with his silk shirt and polished English, we mistook John for an international student from the nearby University of Kentucky. He had a 100-watt smile and eagerly joined in Sunday meals and worship time. Yet as the weeks passed, the complexity of John's life began to emerge. American by birth and the well-educated son of Ghanaian parents, John lived his life under the shadow of schizophrenia. His warmth and sociability overlapped with eccentric requests and stories of passports and identities stolen from him. It was an odd mixture, yet people were naturally drawn to his jaunty stride and pleasant disposition.

Our community did its best to rally around John. Repeated suggestions that he visit the local mental health facility were rebuffed. He claimed that *we* had stolen his passport. He would appear and disappear at random, yet the ties were never severed. We did our best but were often unsure how to proceed.

Then John disappeared and stayed gone. We knew nothing of his whereabouts and heard nothing from folks on the street, and we prayed for John's return to our community. Then one day, leaving his office in a deliberate search for John, my husband

Billy found him sitting on the bench outside. He was living in the basement of a nearby campus chapel where he continued to stay for several months, celebrating with us on Sunday nights and attending an occasional men's small group. It seemed as though things had reached some sense of "normal" until he showed up one Sunday night, disheveled and carrying everything he owned in his backpack. He had left the campus chapel but refused to stay at the local homeless shelter, not an unwise choice for this gentle, fairly well-dressed man with an unusual accent.

What could we do? We allowed him to sleep at our office during the day so that he could stay awake all night in the city parks, but were haunted by the look on his face when he had to leave, especially on Sundays after our time of worship. The joy that normally bathed his features faded, replaced by a disquieting look of dread. Questions were raised, options considered. Can we afford to get him a hotel room? What about transitional housing? His previous subsidized complex refused to allow him back due to an unpaid balance, and he wouldn't hear of it anyway, stating that *they* had taken his passport and "done him wrong." "I have washed my hands of them," he said with a deliberate gesture reminiscent of Pontius Pilate. So we continued to wrestle with the situation, all the time fearing that tomorrow he'd be missing—or dead.

Billy and I were tormented. Surely we couldn't take him into our home, could we? "He smells so bad"—although a shower would fix that. "He's paranoid"—but then, who isn't sometimes? "He hoards things"—well, we have plenty of closet space. "He's homeless"—well, we'd had homeless people crash at our house for a night or two before. Was this different? Friends and respected co-workers reminded us that we couldn't shelter every homeless person that comes our way, while simultaneously affirming our shared commitment to those in need. They asked appropriate and helpful questions about the problems of his living with any of us, questions about personal safety and household security. And always at the end, Billy and I would find ourselves asking, "Will any of this make us feel any better if John dies?" Far from mere middle-class guilt, we finally realized the truth—that John had become our friend, and that it would devastate us if anything happened to him.

It was an unusually heavy summer storm that compelled us to action. As we listened to the rain beating down in swathes, we wondered if John was dry and safe and comfortable, as we were. Finally my husband shook his head. "I can't take this anymore," he said. "Tomorrow I'm going to get him." Together, we knew it was the right decision. We couldn't shelter every homeless person in Lexington, but we could help John. And the following evening, as I prepared what I hoped would be a nice, welcoming meal, the back door opened and in walked John, carrying his backpack. As Billy followed him in, we looked at each other and smiled, not knowing exactly what we had begun, but feeling quite sure that the Lord was smiling too.

Things started off slowly, trying to live this strange new life. While John initially camped out in the dining room, we eventually convinced him that he'd have more privacy in the guest room. We discussed showers, laundry, and eating together regularly; we made sure we were dressed when we walked around the house. However, our slow start quickly picked up steam. When John had been there less than a week, Billy and I had to leave on a previously scheduled trip across the country, and we couldn't find anywhere for him to stay during our absence. Could we leave him there without us? What would he eat? Would it be safe? Would he burn the house down, or move all the canned goods into his closet?

Because we couldn't stand the thought of turning him back onto the street, we (gulp!) decided he could stay. We arranged for people to check on him every day during our absence, stocked the refrigerator, prayed like crazy, and left it in God's and our community's hands. It was an enormous step into the unknown, almost more disquieting than initially inviting him in. And yet, it was this step which began another man's now very intimate and abiding friendship with John; as he checked on him daily, his attitudes towards those in need began to change dramatically.

For the first year, we lived with John and his psychosis. Although seldom belligerent and never violent, John was definitely different. He would cycle through spells of paranoia, often locking himself in his room and refusing to answer; occasionally I would hear him in the bathroom, making himself vomit because he thought I had poisoned him. These times were heartbreaking, though interspersed with growing times of stability and calm. We grew more and more delighted with John's personality, his stories about Ghana and his enjoyment of C-SPAN and the local Christian access channel. "Bill Clinton," he declared, "he is a very smart man, but he loves the women too, too much!" Although we ate few meals together because of his erratic eating habits, we managed to create our own special version of a common life. We brought him to Asbury Seminary's Kingdom Conference where he talked with visiting missionaries; we shared his love for Chinese buffets; we took him to his first movie theater. Life with John was *fun*; we liked living with him. And all the while, the question remained, "So what exactly is the plan for John?"

The problem, however, was that this outlook made John seem more like a project than a person. The real question was: what is God's plan for John, and what role were we to play in that? When he first moved in, many folks stated their hope (and their expectation) that John would get cleaned up, get on medication, get a job, and get an apartment—important steps towards that American ideal, self-sufficiency. However, our community had often critiqued the American model of radical autonomy, stressing instead the communal nature of human life and the need to live in connection with others. If living together was healthy for us "sane" people, then surely it was almost essential for John.

And by all accounts, it was healthy and healing for him as well. People continually remarked on John's improved demeanor, his increased coherence and engagement with others. He began to frequent a local sports bar, watching television and making friends with the wait staff, and he attended other communities' gatherings across the country. We had clearly begun to grow in mutual trust. But the question remained: where is this going? Can he live here forever? What if he never gets better?

Our answer seemed to come one night while we watched the fabulous movie *As Good As It Gets*. As Melvin Udall stormed into his psychiatrist's waiting room and asked, "What if this is as good as it gets?" I looked across the room at John and realized that the question was also ours. What if John never got medicated, never qualified for disability income, never got "better"? Could we continue to live as we had for the past year?

We decided that we could, in faith. We knew there would be much to negotiate, as issues of children and family growth presented themselves, but we trusted in God, our families and friends, and our community to guide us through. It was a decision that made all of us happy. And perhaps it is not surprising that shortly afterwards, John decided to seek psychiatric care through the encouragement of another very important friend who played an indispensable role. He began taking medication and thus began a new chapter of our life together, a chapter both miraculous and miraculously commonplace. We have watched with amazement as John has changed and grown, shedding his psychotic shackles one by one and learning to live in this new world.

It has not always been easy. Reentering a life of sanity after years of untreated mental illness continues to be a difficult transition, and psychiatric medications also bring side effects. Yet from our Christmas card with the three of us by the tree, to our increasingly ordinary arguments over dishes, rent, and cleaning the bathroom, life in our house looks more and more like that of a family. And when we recently asked John if he still wanted to live with us as we prepared to have children, we were delighted when he replied, "Yes. I'd like to stay here, in our home." We look forward to how our children will love and care for John, and to how John will love and care for our children. And as our home has gradually become his home as well, it has been wonderful to see John begin to move from "guest" to "host," from recipient of hospitality to practitioner of it. When we have guests who require welcome, he extends himself alongside Billy and me. And as we begin conversations about the vision for "our house," I look forward to how his voice and his presence will shape that vision.

We realize now, as we have throughout, that we could not have done this by ourselves. Despite his medication, John continues to need a certain level of care and attention, and we rejoice that many people are willing and able to provide it. When we need time to ourselves or go out of town, we can rest in the knowledge that he will be actively included in our community's events. Our care for John is but one aspect of our community's overall care for him, ours being but one of the homes in which he is welcome.

II. Rooting Hospitality in Scripture and Tradition

Our own story of hospitality is but one chapter in the larger Christian narrative, what some have called "the story of God, the story of us."[1] Hopefully, the story is one of faith revealing itself in actions. These actions, which are commonly called Christian practices, are inextricably intertwined with Christian values. Such practices, including prayer, service, and hospitality, serve as both sculptor and sculpture of Christian belief; they both refine and reflect those ideas which our faith regards as true and right and good. In order for our ideas and practices to faithfully reflect God's revelation in the biblical narrative, we must turn to that narrative for their basis. In doing so we can discern foundational roots for the practice of hospitality.

The God Who Welcomes

In every aspect of the Christian life, what we do arises from who we are. And the Christian story makes it clear that who we are is based upon two things: who God is, and who we know ourselves to be in our relationship to him. Thus it is very important to recognize that our God is a God of welcome.

The biblical story is one vast account of God reaching out to

---

[1] "The Story of God, The Story of Us." Sean and Rebecca Gladding, unpublished, 2004.

humanity in tender, abiding love. God created humanity with compassion and purpose and desires our participation in His creation, despite our "otherness" and even our disobedience. If our identity originates in God's identity, then we are also designed to seek connection with others, even those who are "strange" to us. Miroslav Volf, a Croatian theologian who struggled to reconcile with his enemies during the Balkan war, says it well: "God's reception of hostile humanity into divine communion is a model for how human beings should relate to the other."[2] Because we serve a God who welcomes true "strangers" in humanity, we are called—and are able—to welcome our own strangers as well.

This act of connection and welcome is most beautifully seen in the incarnation of God in Christ; when God, as Eugene Peterson's *Message* so clearly describes, "took on flesh and moved into the neighborhood." God took seriously this business of connecting with humanity, so much that he "moved into our neighborhood." This selfless move on the part of God has serious implications for his church. In order to welcome the stranger, one must be near to and available to the stranger. Thus we may also be called to a radical relocation, in order to place ourselves near enough to the "stranger" that such connection is possible.

The fact that we are in relationship with—and in Christ, are actually related to—the God who welcomes not only calls us to follow in his path; it should also give us strength and hope. God has blazed the trail for us, and he will surely accompany us as we follow his lead.

Remembering Ourselves as the Stranger

Who are we? As we saw above, the people of God have a particular character because of particular things—because of who God is and who we are called to be as a result. When we remember our story and our own deliverance from isolation and bondage, we will hear our call to seek out those in loneliness and need,

---

[2] Miroslav Volf, *Exclusion and Embrace: A Theological Exploration of Identity, Otherness, and Reconciliation* (Nashville, TN: Abingdon, 1996), 100.

those who most need comfort and shelter. Because we too were once aliens whom God sought out and welcomed, we will more readily welcome those who are yet strangers.

In Exodus 22:21 and 23:9, God commands Israel to empathize with the strangers among them. "Do not oppress an alien; you yourselves know how it feels to be aliens, because you were aliens in Egypt" (Ex.23:9). Leviticus moves even further, with God instructing Israel to treat the alien "as one of your native-born" (Lev.19:33). Deuteronomy commanded them, after placing their tithe before the Lord's altar, to then give it to the Levite, the alien, the fatherless and the widow (Deut.26:1-15). Throughout the Old Testament, it is clear that mere tolerance is not enough. God exhorts his people to practice active, life-giving care.

The first epistle of Peter further draws on the histories and the identities of the people of God. "But you are a chosen people," claims Peter, "a royal priesthood, a holy nation, a people belonging to God" (1Pet.2:9). Yet he then addresses them as "aliens and strangers in the world" (2:11). In this, Peter illustrates how the church exists simultaneously as chosen and foreign, royal and alien, known in God and unknown in the world. It is our "known-ness" in God which allows, and compels, us to connect with others over our "unknown-ness." We remember the truth of our own welcome by God in Christ, and heed Paul's counsel to "accept one another, then, just as Christ accepted you" (Rom.15:7).

Hospitality as Discipline, Not Gifting

Because it crosses boundaries and calls us out of our comfort zones, hospitality is often regarded as a gifting, as one particular way of being equipped to serve God. However, both the Old and the New Testaments clearly instruct God's people to care for those in need, using imperatives drawn from the language of command rather than gifting. Hospitality is found, not among the spiritual gifts in 1 Corinthians 12, but in what some bibles call the "Conduct for Christian Living" portion of Romans 12. Alongside exhortations to faithful prayer and brotherly love, Paul instructs the church in Rome to "share with God's people who are in need" and "practice hospitality" (Rom.12:13). In language reminiscent of Abraham's hosting the angels in Genesis 18, the author of Hebrews reminds believers: "Do not forget to entertain strangers, for by so doing some people have entertained angels without knowing it" (Heb.13:2). Peter advises us to "offer hospitality to one another without grumbling" (1Pet.4:9). Both Titus and 1 Timothy include hospitality among the requirements for those seeking to be bishops (1Tim.3:2, Tit.1:8).

One of the most compelling descriptions of the practice of hospitality is found in Matthew 25, the well-known story of the sheep and the goats. Interestingly, it comes just after the parable of the talents, in which Jesus commended those who used their resources rather than withholding them. Jesus' account of those who fed the hungry, clothed the naked, cared for the sick, and welcomed the stranger sees their acts of concern for "the least of these" as a direct response to Jesus himself. There is no language of "gifting" here, but rather a clear expectation that those who seek to honor Christ will do so by honoring others.

Initially, some of us may appear more "gifted" at extending hospitality than others. Some homes are more immediately conducive to hosting guests; some personalities are more naturally open to including others. But like prayer and worship, study and fasting, offering hospitality is a spiritual discipline in which we are called—and invited—to learn and to grow.

Welcome as Feast and Celebration

A Pillsbury commercial quips, "Nothing says lovin' like something in the oven," and that says it well. Hospitality is nothing if not the sharing of what sustains us—food, family, and celebration. Christian ethicist Christine Pohl observes, "A shared meal is the activity most closely tied to the reality of God's kingdom, just as it is the most basic expression of hospitality."[3] Far from being

---

[3] Christine Pohl, *Making Room: Recovering Hospitality as a Christian Tradition* (Grand Rapids, MI: Eerdmans, 1999), 30. This book is an indispensable work on the tradition and practice of hospitality. To it I am deeply indebted, and it is my hope that my life and my ministry reflect this.

occasions for mere drudgery, welcoming others should be an occasion for happiness, feasting and joy.

Throughout the biblical narrative, hospitality to the stranger is a consistent and important theme, with meals prominently featured. Abraham welcomed the angels who bore good news for Sarah, and in the heat of the day placed a generous meal before them. (Gen.18:1-15). The widow of Zarephath fed Elijah with apparently supernatural abundance (I Kgs. 17,18). Food is at the center of Jesus' ministry and activity, constantly used to illustrate his message of reconciliation and inclusion. All four Gospels tell of Jesus providing the five thousand with both a spiritual and a physical feast (Mt.14:13-21; Mk.6:30-44; Lk.9:10-17; Jn.6:1-13). He ate many meals with "sinners" such as Zaccheus, thus honoring them and reaffirming their humanity (Lk.19:1-7). When the Prodigal Son returned to his family, his father prepared an extravagant feast to celebrate his virtual "resurrection" (Lk.15:11-32). And it is during a meal with his disciples that Jesus institutes the practice of communion (Mt.26:26-28; Mk.14:22-24; Lk.22:19-20). As we dine together, we participate in the origins of the Eucharist.

Moreover, Christian hospitality always celebrates those who least expect it. In Luke 14, Jesus tells us that when we throw a party, we should especially welcome those folks who cannot return the favor. The poor, the crippled, the lame, the blind—all the people who are pushed to the outskirts of society should be the honored guests. They also deserve to share in the banquet, which is part of the eternal banquet of God's kingdom.

III. Different Ways of Practicing Hospitality

Like prayer, service, and worship, hospitality is not a standardized program, where one set of rules and methods is always appropriate, but a practice in which the entire Christian community participates. Thus the forms which hospitality may assume are as varied as the people that together make up the body of Christ. In order to more fully appreciate the breadth and beauty of existing Christian hospitality, we will consider four different examples of present-day Christian welcome.

Strangers to the Land: Welcoming Refugees at Mercy Street

Mercy Street is a Christian community affiliated with Chapelwood United Methodist Church in Houston, Texas. Their community "forms a mosaic of people diverse in our experiences and backgrounds but common in our desire to seek a closer relationship with God."[4] Over time, they have become connected with people at Interfaith Ministries of Greater Houston (IMGH), who have welcomed and settled refugees in Houston for thirty years. Through these friendships, IMGH asked Mercy Street if they would coordinate the arrival of one family of Somalia Bantu refugees, up to 10,000 of whom would be resettled in the US in the next twelve months. They accepted and thus began the new journey of welcome. In a recent newsletter, one member of Mercy Street recounted the story:

> The Abdullahs, a family of 9, arrived a month ago, but the church that was sponsoring them was unable to follow through on their commitment. Julie asked if we would be willing to welcome them, befriend them, and begin to acculturate them to life in Houston. They arrived with no English, and no concept of life in a developed country. We asked one woman if she would be willing to organize our efforts to love this beautiful family, and she jumped in from day one. She has been amazing in her organizational skills, taking people to meet the family, learning a little Bantu, and her joy and commitment are infectious.

The community of Mercy Street is at once diverse and unremarkable, filled with ordinary people who would not consider themselves specialists in refugee work. Yet through their efforts and compassion, they offer what no government agency could— a network of friends, a community of concern. People who learn another's language, who bring fresh bread or much needed furni-

---

[4] www.mercystreet.org

ture, or take the time to accompany someone on errands provide a powerful witness to the love of God at work in their lives. And the people who embody this love make things possible that would not be possible otherwise. As the above letter concludes, "They are truly enabling our community to welcome the stranger in our midst."

Strangers in the Christian Life: Doing Church at Solomon's Porch

Solomon's Porch is a Christian community in Minneapolis, Minnesota that is "seeking to live the dreams and love of God in the way of Jesus."[5] As an "experimental church," they realize that their relationships with God "are not limited to what we officially do in our meeting space, but are expressed through our lives." For their community, hospitality is a central means by which this expression takes place. This hospitality includes regular meals but goes beyond them as well.

> Our hospitality is not limited to meals. It's really about involvement and the act of welcoming the stranger. The real point of this brand of hospitality is the spiritual forma-tion that takes place when we share the rhythm of regular life with one another...at the same time, hospitality is about welcoming the outsider, the needy, and those from whom we are disconnected.[6]

For Solomon's Porch, hospitality is a way of drawing out and drawing in, of allowing people to share of themselves and their journeys with God, and then bringing them and their experiences together with others in the family of faith. "When stories are shared," says pastor Doug Pagitt, "individual experiences become communal experiences. This is hospitality at its most profound."

Becoming the family of God is harder than it seems. In our

---

[5] www.solomonsporch.com

[6] Doug Pagitt, *Reimagining Spiritual Formation: A Week in the Life of an Ex-perimental Church* (El Cajon, CA: emergent YS, 2003), 104.

highly individualized culture, we are not used to forming such intimate relationships and deep commitments with others. And when we welcome others into our lives and begin to share their burdens, we assume the risk of feeling and bearing their pain as well. "Yet it is precisely this risk that makes hospitality a meaningful element of spiritual formation in the Christian life," says Pagitt. "In these times we find the call to live the invitational life of our crucified Savior both heart-wrenching and life-encouraging."

Strangers Sharing Lives: Living Together in L'Arche Communities

L'Arche (French for "The Ark") is an international association of communities filled with "people with a learning disability and those who choose to share their lives."[7] It was founded by Jean Vanier, a former officer in the Canadian Navy and professor of philosophy, and two men, Raphael Simi and Philippe Seux, who were living in an institution outside Paris. Aware that they "could not help everyone, but that by helping a few, together they might be a sign to others," Vanier, Raphael and Philippe began living the new life of L'Arche, a life dedicated to "combining spirituality and humanity."

Life in L'Arche homes is "simple and family-like," says the community's website, and "each person has a role to play in their shared life." Members of L'Arche move beyond the one-way street of the typical patient-assistant relationship and into a deeply reciprocal experience of genuine growth.

> Assistants in L'Arche are not there primarily to "do things" for people with learning disabilities, but to become their friends, their brothers and sisters. We are bound together by a covenant of love; we are members of the same family… This covenant journey is an opportunity to grow for each one of us.

---

[7] All quotes from www.larche.org.

These assistants clearly see the profound changes wrought by their way of life. "This encounter does not leave us untouched," one said. "If we take the risk of entering into a relationship with a person who has learning disabilities, of listening to their suffering, of becoming their friend, then something within us is transformed. Our vision changes."

Despite their growth to 130 communities in 29 countries, Vanier continues to remind others of an even larger vision. "We're just a tiny part of a wider movement to reveal the value of people who are weak and broken, to reveal the 'power' of the weak, their capacity to transform other people," he says.

We are just part of the announcing of a vision of human beings, a vision of the body of humanity, of Jesus and the Church."

Strangers to Being Strangers: Receiving Hospitality from Another

My friend Sherry met Omid as she weeded her vegetable garden. A Kurdish Iraqi living in Lexington with her husband and daughter, Omid immediately welcomed Sherry, her husband, and the rest of our community into her home as naturally as if we were family. She fed us enormous and tasty Middle Eastern meals, visited new mothers to give comfort and advice, and participated with her husband in our community's mourning and conversation after the September 11th attacks and before the bombing of Baghdad. In a culture where she was officially the "stranger," she offered the most gracious of welcomes to everyone she met.

As we saw earlier, Israel's remembrance of itself as alien and stranger in Egypt was essential to its identity and behavior. As Americans, however, we have largely forgotten what it's like to be a stranger. With our massive borders and relative isolation, we have lost touch with the sense of our own vulnerability. We imagine ourselves to be, like the Laodicean church in the book of Revelation, "rich and in need of nothing" (Rev.3:17). Yet like the Laodiceans and people everywhere, we are also "wretched, pitiful, poor, blind and naked," and we may realize this most clearly when we allow ourselves to be welcomed by others.

It is rarely easy. Christine Pohl notes in *Making Room*, "Persons who have never experienced need or marginality, or who are uncomfortable with their own vulnerability, often find it easier to be hosts than guests." Often our unwillingness to recognize another's ability to help us leads us to reject the role of guest in favor of the more comfortable and powerful role of host, as allowing others to care for us recognizes and validates their contributions and worth. To let someone welcome us is to say, "I believe you have something that will help me. You are in charge here, and I trust you and commit myself into your care." For people who exist on the periphery of society, this recognition is enormously empowering. When we welcome refugees, share homes and lives with the learning disabled, or meet new neighbors across the tomato patch, we must make room for the gifts and blessings they are eager to share.

Ultimately, it is Jesus who is our model for both guest and host. He who serves as the eternal Host of the Eucharist was also the guest of tax collectors and "sinners." If he was able to receive care and welcome from others, then surely we should do so as well.

The Simple Goodness of Hospitality

If these tales seem a bit "run of the mill," it might be because they are, indeed, quite ordinary. Often the richest and most abiding stories of hospitality are the ones lived out quietly but with great faithfulness. One person reflected back on his childhood:

> In recent years I have come to realize that without fanfare my parents practiced hospitality throughout their lives. That is the way it is with the practice of hospitality. If someone really makes his or her home your home, there really is nothing spectacular about it.[8]

---

[8] Jonathan Wilson, *Gospel Virtues: Practicing Faith, Hope & Love in Uncertain Times* (Downers Grove, IL: InterVarsity, 1998), 163.

Welcoming the stranger often resembles the wedding at Cana, with Jesus turning the water into wine. When the Lord is present and the people are willing, the most common parts of our lives are transformed into instruments of blessing and celebration.

Throughout the journey of the last two years, Billy, John and I have made many beautiful memories; yet one always stands out, unremarkable in itself but perhaps the best illustration of the change that God has wrought in us. One evening, John stood at the stove cooking rice for dinner while I flipped channels on TV and finally settled on "Friends," which John and I occasionally watch together. As the opening credits ran, John whistled and I sang along, "I'll be there for you, when the rain starts to fall." And John looked up from the stove and smiled at me. "Those people," he said, "they are friends, just like us."

Hospitality? Yes. To a stranger? Not anymore.

Mark 4: Lament for Racial Divisions Within the Church and Our Communities Combined with the Active Pursuit of a Just Reconciliation

Chris Rice

I. A New Racial Time

Given that St. Benedict and Martin Luther King are not normally mentioned in the same breath, it is highly significant, and somewhat odd, that Christians who identify a set of practices shaping a new monasticism would dare to name "lamenting racial divisions" as a defining mark. What is at stake in such a claim? For in America today it is no small achievement to genuinely lament racial divisions. Racism may be America's "original sin," but forty years after legal desegregation it is not immediately evident that there *is* such a thing as racial division that calls the church to grieve.

We live in a new and fuzzier racial time. An entire generation has no memory of the civil rights movement and little interest in looking back. Across racial lines, many people suspect the white racism glove doesn't fit like it used to.[1] In examining social prob-

---

[1] The litany of African Americans voicing such a claim are hardly "conservatives," and include William Raspberry, Bill Cosby, Hugh Price (formerly of the Urban League), rising Democrat star Barack Obama, and Kwame Mfume of the NAACP. The force of white racism today is an issue of enormous debate. But even this public debate, especially among African Americans, is a new dynamic.

lems that continue to disproportionately face minority communities (i.e. violence, AIDS, family break-down, incarceration, etc.), the lines between economic forces, racial injustice, and personal responsibility are not as easy to detect as during segregation. Simple categories of "race," "black," and "white" have become more complex with the language of "ethnicity" and burgeoning post-1960s arrivals of new immigrants, especially Asians and Latinos. A large black middle-class has been born, and for decades now black folk have been moving out of the old neighborhoods. African Americans have even had enough time to prove that their churches are just as capable of neglecting the poor as white Christians. In laying out the greater fuzziness of racial discernment today, I am not trying to suggest any quick conclusions. I *am* arguing that a new racial time in America calls for deeper diagnosis in order to see what compels us to lament.

Nothing brings this home better than the situation in the American church. To accept there is something as serious as "racial division" that infects my congregation would be to admit that something has gone very wrong ecclesially, both locally and nationally, in who our members are or how we think about and relate to churches of a different ethnic stripe or the very contours of our patterns of worship, theology, relationship, and mission. But the truth is, most Christians don't see their church in the grip of forces of racialization. These days I find myself not only trying to convince whites, but African Americans and other people of color, that it is a serious problem that 95% or more of white American Christians worship in all-white congregations and 90% of African Americans worship in all-black.[2]

The vast number of American churches, whether consciously or not, *are* ethnic-specific. How should this on-going existence of different church worlds be named? Is it a sign of diversity and "cultural preference" to be celebrated—the gifts of different worship styles, finding a church that's comfortable for me, a spiritual refuge of familiar songs, liturgies, even beats on which we clap?

---

[2] Michael Emerson, *Divided by Faith* (Oxford University Press, 2000), p. 16.

Is it an innocent matter of preferring to share the Christian life with people like me, doing no harm to others? Or do we name these different worlds as a segregated Sabbath, a sign of deep-seated racialization and division? Who wants to see their Sunday worship service as *that,* as if we have seriously missed the mark of what it means to be the church?

II. What Do We Lament?

A closer look at two particular churches offers a deeper diagnosis. For 100 years, Blacknall Memorial Presbyterian, our family's church home in Durham, North Carolina, has sat on the west side of Broad Street. Blacknall's membership is almost entirely white. Just six blocks east across Broad Street, with powerful Duke University's campus near each congregation, sits St. John's Missionary Baptist Church, which also has a 100-year history. But St. John's is almost entirely African American.[3]

Two congregations, one essentially white, one essentially black, separated for a hundred years by a few blocks, never prayed or studied Scripture together, entered each other's sanctuaries of worship, became close friends, sponsored a common program or mission, or even shared a meal, until very recently. Why? If all Christians make up one family, how could brothers and sisters in such close vicinity never have imagined reaching out to fellow family members? If such a condition of separateness calls for lament, why? Were Blacknall and St. John's simply celebrating our diversity all these years, or were our separate worlds determined and shaped by more insidious forces?

It is crucial to place the two churches within a larger context, because Broad Street represents, I believe, a microcosm of America's racialized divisions. Broad Street is not innocent. It di-

---

[3] I will use "black" and "white" and focus on Blacknall, St. John's, and Walltown as racial shorthand, knowing full well that inside of Blacknall are a few Asian-American and African-American members, and that Durham's and America's wider terrain is far more complex. Receive my analysis as an analogy, not an exhaustive commentary on race in America.

vides two different worlds that have been almost completely iso-lated for a hundred years as people, as communities, and as church—worlds which continue to be divided. While many won-derful things have happened at both Blacknall and St. John's in their years, Broad Street must be named a border, a racial and economic boundary birthed in hostilities and carrying out trajec-tories of division, with a long history that has entangled the lives of Christians and their churches.

Across Broad Street around St. John's is the vibrant life of all-black and Latino Walltown, where people hang out in the evenings on front porches and children play in the streets. The Walltown neighborhood includes both stable working families and people who line up for the food bank every other Friday. New Latino immigrant "strangers" live next door to elderly black folks who have lived in Walltown their entire lives, from wise "prayer war-rior" church ladies to the gentleman I befriended one summer who quickly admitted, "Yeah, I been drinking, what about it?"

Crossing Broad Street again, the essentially white neighbor-hood around Blacknall where my family resides appears to be thriving, with a booming small business district, rising housing values, and nobody lining up for food giveaways. Parents trans-port children to a constant stream of schools, lessons, and activities. Surely our neighborhood is full of problems and addictions, but they are mostly well-hidden or socially acceptable. If someone on my side of Broad Street was addicted, I'm not sure how I would find out.

While we appear to have life under control, many Walltown residents openly admit the existence of powers gripping their lives: the drug business and the fear and gunshots it can bring at night, the economic and university powers they fear intend to gentrify the community and push out long-time residents. Many have faith in God without having social power, which is no small gift to the church. *We* in my neighborhood mostly fear going onto Walltown turf, and certainly wouldn't choose to live there unless maybe we discerned God speaking (it happens). *They* mostly don't come onto our turf, and couldn't afford to live here.

Hear the language: *We. They. Us. Them.* Behind those categories and their different patterns is a history of powerful and powerless, Duke and Walltown, insiders and outsiders, racial and class dynamics, separation and alienation living on in quieter ways. *We. They. Us. Them.* These trajectories have also led Christians in very different directions. The lives of churches do not run in a pure, separate historical stream, but are carried on inside of and tainted by the world's poisoned, muddy histories. It has simply never occurred to anyone now at St. John's to join Blacknall, or vice versa. It is simply and unconsciously assumed that one is an exclusively black space, the other an exclusively white space. Nor have Blacknall and St. John's people ever lived side by side, sharing neighborhood life. These imaginations and patterns, now taken for granted, emerged within a larger landscape of political and ecclesial histories. America's church patterns of "us" and "them" were and continue to be indelibly shaped by trajectories birthed in legal segregation and church schisms that had very little to do with housing preferences or worship styles, and everything to do with race, white supremacy, and slavery.

Racialized divisions in America have become, in Wendell Berry's phrase, a "hidden wound," marked not by open hostility but by normalization within racialized, divided, accepted patterns of life concerning who "our people" are. Like the divide between Jew and Gentile, Broad Street is a boundary that has come to be accepted on *both sides* as normal and acceptable, even inevitable. Gentiles were *them,* not *us. Those people,* not *our people. Other* and *alien,* not *family.* To lament and grieve the trajectories that separate Blacknall and St. John's as emblematic of racial divisions in America is to attempt to faithfully illuminate what is hidden and proclaim what is not.

III. Lament as Remembering and Grieving Well

If I am right that Broad Street must be named a divide, a symbolic and hidden "dividing wall of hostility" (Eph. 2:14), and that the communities and churches on either side have been profoundly shaped by a deep and hidden racial wound, then some crucial observations emerge about truthful lament and America's racial divisions.

First, essentially black and white churches, Broad Street divides, and different communal ways of being did not drop like meteors from the sky. The ground on which we live is not innocent; it only seems so because of forgetfulness. The histories and trajectories of schisms, social divisions, and racialization have, to a large extent, become normalized. Racial separateness has come to seem normal, acceptable, even inevitable, to the extent that we do not question, much less *see,* how deeply our churches and life patterns have been formed by race and economics.

Secondly, lament thus becomes a practice and task of remembering and grieving well, through which Christians do not forget and continue naming the truth about the past. To the extent communities of Christians are able to do this, lament is not only a cry of grief—"Oh, God, we see and feel the pain of our divides, our brokenness!"—but a declaration of hope—"This is *not* the way God intends things to be! Christ brings new life!" Through faithful lament of racial divisions, perhaps even little communities shaped by a new monasticism will one day protect lost truth like those few ancient monasteries which once sheltered great texts of western civilization which otherwise would have been forgotten. Tamed by a national holiday, Dr. King is in danger of becoming remembered as merely a dreamer of "black and white together." It is no small thing to keep the memory of King alive as an Amos-like prophet of the church naming sins of militarism, racism, and materialism, abandoned by many after publicly opposing the Vietnam War. Prophetic communities that remember well become a sign of hope.

Thirdly, what comes into view is that as we pursue holiness, we are also called to do the hard work of social analysis. Behind faithful lament is theological and social discernment. These skills will make other divisions in our churches and communities visible, between men and women, privileged and marginalized. The schisms and trajectories of race have made some powerful claims in deforming the American church, but so have tragic schisms between Orthodox, Catholic, and Protestant. Such divisions also call for deep theological and social discernment and lament.

A fourth crucial point concerns how racial division should be discerned in relationship to cultural differences, or "celebrating diversity." Difference itself is not necessarily the problem, and is to be distinguished from division. God created a world full of glorious difference, and diversity can be a gift through cultures which enrich life and connect us deeply to others through common traditions. We are creatures who live embodied lives on particular ground in particular places, and differences that emerge in language and cultural practices can be celebrated. But not without openness to theological examination from the standpoint of life in a fallen world and its estrangement from God's intentions. Like America's glut of ethnic- and class-specific churches, cultures do not drop from the sky. They are formed through histories. Because all histories are disordered with forces of domination, brokenness, and sin, cultures cannot be taken for granted. Diversity as an end in itself easily becomes ethnocentrism as an end in itself—a closed community or church, living a fallacy of self-sufficiency, disabled from self-criticism, limiting life to "people like us."

The way "people like us" begins to become examined is through our openness and hospitality to the stranger, to people *not like us*—to the neighbor I have not loved (e.g. people in Walltown), the alien in my midst, the enemy across the divide, the least of these, the orphan, the widow, the prisoner. Calls to these practices are deeply embedded in Scripture. Israel is only Israel in being "a light to the nations," and the church is only the church in being witnesses "to the ends of the earth" (Acts 1:8). Openness and hospitality to the stranger are a check against culture (or cultural preference, or the church as a personal refuge) becoming an end in itself. Such openness puts our identity at risk, for we cannot remain the same in the exchange. What are we going to do with that homeless guy if he keeps showing up for our worship service, and starts to bring his friends? What if that group of starry-eyed white folks keeps coming to our African-American church, and shows up at choir practice? What if they move into our neighborhood, and we find ourselves moved into theirs? And the worst of all fears for many: what if *their* boys start to get interested in *our* girls?

So what *will* happen as we reach out across divides to the stranger? Mess will surface, both personal and institutional, mess that we'll have to cry out for the Holy Spirit to touch and heal. Who "our people" are will begin to change, bringing a mixture of joy and fear as strangers become companions. Through a continual interplay of God's grace and our perseverance, small signs of hope will begin to break in, giving glimpses that the way things are is not the way things have to be. Our vision of transformation will begin to change as we see that the depth of social division and how it has infected our world is deeper than we imagined. We will begin to see that pursuit of a just reconciliation is a long and costly process, requiring forgiveness, patience, and hope, nurtured in practices of listening to God. In short, what will happen in the exchange with the stranger is that a whole new set of challenges will emerge through which we will have to learn how to be the church.

It is, indeed, an achievement and gift to faithfully lament racial divisions. In doing so, we have become able to name certain powers that grip us, and to recognize what has pushed us and somehow sticks us complacently onto different sides of the Broad Street divides. And now we *see* certain people we have never seen, people who matter to us for the first time. We see the stranger we are called to go to and offer hospitality. We see the brother or sister we have never imagined praying with. And we go pray with them.

IV. Some Concrete Challenges in Pursuing a Just Reconciliation

What would it mean for the Christians on both sides to live as if there is no Broad Street divide, but only the one, holy, catholic church confessed in the Apostles' Creed? At stake here is surely not tolerance or political correctness, but the Holy Spirit disrupting and transforming us. Central to the story of the church in Acts are two themes: the power of the Holy Spirit in the risen Christ, and the formation of a profound new community across lines of language, ethnicity, and privilege. If Jesus has been crucified and is risen from the dead, the world has been turned upside down. There is no more social life as usual. We are a people who know that who we eat and pray with and seek a just reconciliation with names who "our people" are.

A just reconciliation regarding historic and abiding racial divisions cannot be grabbed or mandated. Yet we pledge ourselves to seek to pursue and embody signs of hope. Some concrete challenges arise in attending to this with respect to the vision and practices of a new monasticism.

One challenge is to remain deeply unsatisfied with a monologue with "people like us." This dissatisfaction will seek authentic dialogical encounter toward a far more transformative conversation and diversity of holy friendships. For example, to call for dialogue around a new monasticism only rings bells for people with a certain kind of tradition, or network, or education. It assumes there's something attractive about renewing something called "monasticism," but does nothing for (and may repel) others for whom it might evoke a vague image of a thin, robed, white guy chanting inside distant, dark walls with other thin, robed, white guys, far removed from the streets, the world's pain, and a prophetic voice to the status quo. But how needful it is today to think across divides, to have imaginative encounters such as between the traditions of Benedict and of Dr. King! Such an encounter is itself a sign of hope. Becoming dialogical requires far more than "build it—or say it—and they will come," but going out of our way to engage new and uncomfortable conversation partners, guided into unfamiliar places by the question, "Since I believe the Holy Spirit is at work enabling the church to recover certain practices, where is the Spirit at work doing this among Christians of color? Where are the signs of hope within those traditions and communities?"

Pursuing a just reconciliation also involves missional solidarity with other Christians and with people of good will, without compromising our Christian convictions. Never far from Blacknall and St. John's and engaging our historic divide via ecclesial and relational encounter should be the priority of engaging the Walltown neighborhood together. Jesus embodied a distinctive love for and identified special gifts within the feared and endangered places, the Samarias, the outcasts, and the ones who know they are sinners. Concentrated places of people forgotten on the margins remind us that reconciliation is not only a personal and relational pursuit, but involves active social and prophetic engagement, joining with Christians and people of good will to discern and advocate for just practices, comfort and bind up the afflicted, partner in seeking community transformation, and join in mutual life with "the least of these." It may surprise us to learn how much our own transformation is at stake.

At the same time, pursuing a just reconciliation always brings us back home. There is a great temptation toward utilitarianism: to favor "doing" over "being," to become determined by an insistence on wide and visible impacts and the "how-to's" that supposedly get you there, to energetically address what seems "big" (the neighborhood, city, nation) over seeking small signs of hope and addressing the patterns of my own little life and Christian community. Unlearning the hidden habits of racism, ethnocentrism, and exclusion begins at home. This brings us to some difficult challenges concerning the membership of Christian communities who tend to be attracted to a new monasticism.

For 12 years I was a member of an interracial Christian community called Antioch in an urban neighborhood in Jackson, Mississippi. We shared a big 12-bedroom house, a common purse and refrigerator, daily meals around a table that sat 16, and a common life of Christian friendship and mission. Our motto was, "There's always room for one more." Antioch welcomed all kinds of strangers to our table and life: ex-cons, unwed mothers, eager-beaver college students.

While we had an equal number of blacks and whites as founding members, far more new white folks wanted to join us. One of our leaders and black members, Spencer Perkins, often told us, "Way more whites are going to be attracted to this." Spencer was right not only about Antioch, but about recent post-1960s traditions of faithful Protestant American communities of deep commitment to the poor, reconciliation, and radical communal sharing. From Sojourners in Washington D.C. to Reba Place in Chicago to Koinonia in rural Georgia, these communities tried very hard, and largely failed, to recruit members of color.

Spencer's theory was that educated whites who came from family histories of social privilege, and had come to see the dead end of materialism and the "rat race," were now willing to mobilize downward. But African American life was on a very different trajectory, coming from the margins into new educational and economic possibilities, mobilizing upward. Before we started Antioch, I lived in the local urban neighborhood as a church member with white roommates who were determined to eat regular meatless meals, not use air conditioning, and live what we called a "simple lifestyle." What a shock to see my new black Antioch housemates insist on "air" and ask "where's the meat" when a casserole appeared on the table. (At the New Monasticism gathering, after one panel member spoke of the value of organic farming, an African American panelist who grew up poor exclaimed, "That's all *we* had growing up, an organic farm!") Having lived without historical benefits, the black folks at Antioch were ready to test and enjoy. And the truth was, there *was* a power differential; if things at Antioch fell apart, we whites had major resources and options to fall back on that the black members had not had enough time or social justice to gain—educational degrees, financial capital, moneyed family and networks.

Antioch's black members gave our community the gift of not taking "radical discipleship" so seriously, of bringing a certain joyful lightheartedness to life together. But in discerning a just reconciliation, the undercurrent of power must be grappled with. Dr. King is reported to have once said, "We don't want to be integrated out of power, but into power." It is crucial, I believe, that the Antioch Community was birthed *after* a racial crisis in the larger congregation we were all part of, a showdown over issues of white privilege—like why our various ministry projects were nearly all managed by whites, and why the church elder board was similarly constituted. The racial crisis was about trust and power, and the interrelationship between the two. Moving from power, you carry more guilt and are more interested in gaining relationship and trust; moving from the margins, you carry more interest in changing the status quo and addressing issues of power, without which you believe you cannot trust.

Jesus took power very seriously, transforming it and using power as a suffering servant. This is one theological standpoint from which power should be interrogated. Having said that, a danger for those with power moving downward is to not recognize the role of certain options in making their vision and downward mobility possible. Among many other ingredients, it is not in spite of education, but certainly partly *because of it,* that leadership emerges with the skills to lead. People who found and lead these communities of intense discipleship tend to be highly-educated, having had the opportunity and leisure to read books which stirred their conscience and imagination, study the church's history (e.g. "monasticism"), develop intellectual capital and skills in thinking, writing, persuading, administering, and transforming. We dare not name privilege or privileged ways of knowing as a necessity for faithful leadership (thereby excluding the possibility of a Fannie Lou Hamer and countless anonymous others), but neither must we be naïve to think that becoming empowered in certain ways does not matter; Dorothy Day was well-educated, Dr. King had a PhD, and Gandhi and Mandela were highly-trained lawyers. At the very same time, power remains a demonic temptation. With greater economic progress, any people become subject to the insatiable desire for increasing consumer goods, attaching God's will to greater material prosperity, and gaining more and more control over life such that faith in God becomes less and less of a reality. This is, indeed, a tricky terrain of discernment and negotiation, learning to stick together in the intersection of ones moving from power and others moving from the margins.

Again and again, we must be called back to our hope in God. At the initial New Monasticism gathering, I was invited to speak to racial challenges. I directed some of my comments to exploring why the communities which were currently being drawn to such a vision, while often embedded in multi-ethnic communities, are essentially white in membership, and the task of changing this reality.

During the response time, a friend who is a committed member of an urban Christian community said, "Chris, I don't know whether to thank you or not. We have worked so hard to make this happen." As he told some of his community's history and struggle, it was clear his heart was broken, that he would do whatever it took.

We talked afterwards. I said, "To be deeply bothered is a sign of hope." I wanted him to hear that we are not in control of reconciliation. I wanted to explode the activism which too often drives Christians who think that by trying harder and doing more our Christian communities can become all they should be. "We have to keep proclaiming what is not, even what is not in our own midst," I said. "Even if things never really change." This does far more than keep us open to transformation. Proclaiming what is not keeps calling us to hope in God, to humility, to resist certainty, self-congratulation, and the pride which so easily besets self-proclaimed "radical disciples."

It is exactly right to put "lamenting racial divisions" in front of "pursuing a just reconciliation." Lament reminds us that we are not God, that visions like the new monasticism do not capture the Kingdom, that true reconciliation is only in the eschaton, when all things are reconciled in Christ. We keep naming the "not yet" of the coming Kingdom, keep praying to be interrupted by the unexpected, keep reaching out to the stranger, keep holding our hands outward for the gift of new people that the Holy Spirit may bring us tomorrow. Or not.

Mark 5: Humble Submission to Christ's Body, the Church

Ivan Kauffman

I. Amish Roots, Catholic Home

For some 300 years all my ancestors in the male line have been Amish or Mennonite. One of my distant forbears was a founder of the Amish. Although the Amish are now known for their conservative ways, in seventeenth-century Switzerland when they began they were the epitome of radical Christian discipleship. They set out to create a new way of life, one in which ordinary lay persons with families would live out the Gospel without compromise.

The Amish had actually broken away from another movement of radical Christian intentionality that began in the sixteenth century—the Swiss Anabaptists as they are now known to historians, or the Brethren as they called themselves, or the *Taufer* (the German word for Baptist) as their neighbors called them. We are now coming to understand that both these movements had their origins in medieval monasticism, and were an attempt to take that thousand-year-old pattern and make it workable for people who were not celibate.

Both the early Anabaptists and the early Amish made enormous sacrifices in living out this vision—many of them paying with their lives, others being forced into exile, and some even sold as galley slaves. Those who escaped these terrible punishments suffered severe discrimination that continued for centuries. They could not own land in Europe, and to survive had to be ready to move at a moment's notice. They were among the first immigrants to America in the early 1700s.

But they did survive, proving that married people with families can live out the Gospel—including its command to love one's enemies without qualification, which for them meant giving up the right to self-defense in all cases. In many ways this story could be the beginning of what is now called the new monasticism. It is an inspiring story, one that is increasingly being recognized by both Protestants and Catholics as worthy of great respect.

But by the time I arrived on the scene in the late 1930s, what had begun as an experiment in radical discipleship had become something very close to a legalistic tribal religion. Although the early Anabaptists and Amish had been intensely evangelistic, their successors had given this up as the price of survival and the movement they had founded now consisted of small groups of inter-related families living in rural areas across North America. The dream had survived, but it had come to be embodied in an ethnic group that followed a strict set of rules—an unwritten, oppressive rule that governed every aspect of human life.

Many of these rules were consistent with the original dream—especially the rule that no member of the community could serve in the armed forces—but others were merely arbitrary, especially the rules that governed the way members of the community dressed. As a result more and more of the community's energies were poured into simply maintaining the status quo. The fear was that if anything changed everything would change, and the community would simply assimilate into mainstream society and lose its identity.

From this vantage point we saw the wider church as a threat, not a resource. Frequently even other Mennonite congregations were suspect because they did things slightly differently. Our own congregations were a threat because their very existence was constantly in danger of being destroyed by an ugly church fight, often over some trivial matter, like the details of the plain clothing we required ourselves to wear. What had begun as a movement based on deep personal faith and the power of grace had become a guarded institution which relied on the power of individual wills.

We did not know it but we were repeating a pattern that has recurred throughout church history. There are examples of will-based legalism in every Christian century, but the particular instance which has given this belief its name occurred in the fifth century, when a monk from England named Pelagius began teaching the doctrine that salvation depends on how hard we try. The great theologian of the time, Augustine of Hippo, immediately saw how unrealistic this idea was, and refuted it with arguments that Christians throughout the centuries since have found convincing.

Even though we were once again proving the futility of Pelagius' teachings (and the realism of Augustine's arguments against them), we had no way of knowing this since we were cut off from the church's past. We were so sure we were right that it would have seemed dangerous to learn from other Christians—either those now living or those who had lived in the past.

Growing up in this environment produced a very serious personal crisis in my early twenties. It was becoming increasingly obvious that I could not live up to the extremely high ethical standards that my tradition had taught me, but I could not give them up either. Either way I felt lost. It all seemed so impossible; I was close to suicide.

In the midst of that terrible crisis, I discovered what I would now call the Great Tradition. It is the set of beliefs and practices that have been maintained by Christians throughout the centuries and are still held by the vast majority of Christians. Not everyone who is part of the Great Tradition believes everything in it of course; but everything that Christians do agree on is part of it.

What saved my life was the discovery that this ancient body of belief exists, that it has been tested and assented to by millions of people throughout the ages, and that I could adopt it as the intellectual and spiritual foundation for my life. The impossible burden of having to do it all by myself and the terrible insecurity of never knowing if I was right were both lifted from my shoulders. A new life opened before me. I now saw the church as a gift rather than an accomplishment. With that realization a life-long process of conversion began, slowly changing me from someone who relied entirely on his own efforts into someone who accepted the gifts of grace that are all about us. I have come to find the meaning of life in passing these gifts on to others, especially the poorest of the poor.

II. The Church in Scripture and Tradition

The Christian churches are currently divided between two very different understandings of the church. In short we can say that some Christians hold that we become Christians by joining the church, whereas others hold that we create the church by becoming Christians. One group emphasizes the religious experience of the individual in the present, the other emphasizes the importance of the church as a human community in history.

For St. Paul this distinction between personal belief and church membership did not exist. For him they were two sides of a single coin. It was obvious that without personal conversion it is impossible to be a Christian, but that it is just as impossible to be a Christian without being part of the church. No one has ever seen the need for personal conversion more clearly than Paul, but neither has anyone ever seen the role of the church in our conversions more clearly. Paul's great vision of the body of Christ, which has inspired the Christian community for almost 2,000 years, sees each Christian as part of a living whole—an organism that like the human body consists of many very different parts, each of which makes some vital contribution to the whole, and each of which benefits from the contributions of the other parts. We are not merely marbles in a bucket—autonomous beings who happen to be in the same place at the same time, each of whom are capable of living whole and healthy lives by themselves. We are cells in a body, each giving something to the body which it needs and each receiving from the other cells in that body what we need to sustain our lives.

This image of the church appears again and again in Paul's letters. To the Romans he writes, "For as in one body we have many parts, and all the parts do not have the same function, so we, though many, are one body in Christ and individually parts of one another" (Rom.12:4,5). To the Corinthians he wrote, "God has so constructed the body as to give greater honor to a part that is without it, so that there may be no division in the body, but that the parts may have the same concern for one another. If one part suffers, all the parts suffer with it; if one part is honored, all the parts share its joy" (I. Cor.12:24b-26).

Paul's vision of the church as the living body of Christ has its fullest expression in the letter to the Ephesians, where he writes,

"And he gave to some as apostles, others as prophets,
others as evangelists,
others as pastors and teachers,
to equip the holy ones for the work of ministry,
for building up the body of Christ,
until we all attain to the unity of faith and knowledge of
  the Son of God,
to mature personhood, to the extent of the full stature of
  Christ,
so that we may no longer be infants,
tossed by waves and swept along by every wind of teaching...
Rather, living the truth in love,
we should grow in every way into him who is the head,
  Christ,
from whom the whole body,
joined and held together by every supporting ligament,
with the proper functioning of each part,
brings about the body's growth and builds itself up in love"
  (Eph.4:11-16).

The early Christians saw this relationship between the individual believer and the gathered community as so important that they said, "Outside the church there is no salvation." By this they did not mean that the church somehow magically dispenses salvation. What they meant was that it is in the personal formation and the ongoing conversion which our regular participation in the activities of the gathered church requires and makes possible that we become mature Christians. Without that experience we do not become mature Christians. Cyprian of Carthage, one of the pre-Constantinian martyrs, wrote, "One cannot have God as a father who doesn't have the church as a mother."

It has always been a great temptation for especially fervent Christians to think that they are so superior to other Christians of lesser commitment that they do not need to associate with them. But to succumb to this temptation is to fall prey to the greatest sin of all, the sin of pride—and to the worst form of pride, which is spiritual pride. When that great evil enters our lives, as it does in every Christian's life at some point, we lose any sense of needing others. We lose any capacity to learn from others, any chance of having our faults corrected by others, and any hope of serving them since everyone quickly senses spiritual pride and is repulsed by it.

The people in Jesus' time who were most affected by this great evil were the Pharisees, a group of especially committed religious persons whose attitude toward everyone else in their faith community was indicated by the name of their party, a word which means *separate*. Of all the sins that existed in Jesus' day, this is the one he condemned most strongly. The Pharisees' attempts to follow the law more strictly did not make them better followers of Moses and the Prophets. Instead, it made them into hypocrites and self-centered individuals who cared only about themselves and their own welfare. They were inauthentic people whose external appearances did not match their true inner lives. Of these people Jesus said, "They preach but they do not practice...they love places of honor at banquets, seats of honor in synagogues…[they] cleanse the outside of cup and dish, but inside they are full of plunder and self-indulgence…[they] appear righteous, but inside … are filled with hypocrisy and evildoing."

The only alternative to the twin evils of individualism and spiritual pride is a "humble submission to Christ's body, the church." Despite their faults—and they are many—every Christian congregation and every Christian denomination nevertheless has within it Christ's living presence. It is not easy for radically committed persons to see themselves as part of these very imperfect structures and to participate in them as accountable members. But unless we do our efforts will come to nothing, for Christ has chosen to be present to us in the church, and unless we accept his presence there we will find him nowhere.

That may not be our choice, but it is Christ's choice, and if we want to follow him we will have to take our place among his other followers. Even when our place in the church is to make a radical witness to discipleship, which often requires criticizing the church's present practices, we are nevertheless part of the church we seek to reform.

When the monastic movement was emerging on the Egyptian desert 1,700 years ago, one of the early monks had a dream. He saw a large group traveling in the desert at night without a road. In the distance they could see a light they were traveling toward, but they could not see how to reach it. However, these people believed there were persons in front of them who were able to see the light and how to reach it, and so they had each placed their hands on the shoulder of the person ahead of them, in an unbroken line reaching to the front. So long as they stayed connected in this way they were safe.

But a few persons thought this procedure was too limiting. And so they announced they knew a better way to reach the light and promised that if others followed them they would reach the light more quickly and more easily. And so small groups would break off and follow these persons. But soon these small groups found themselves hopelessly lost, wandering around in circles in the desert. And then these small groups would in turn split up into even smaller groups, each disagreeing with the others and each seeking to find the light on its own.

The early monks remembered this vision and eventually wrote it down because it encapsulated their relationship to the church. The Benedictine monasticism that eventually emerged in Europe maintained an existence very distinct from the wider church, but at the same time always saw itself as part of the church. As a result the medieval monastic movement fed the wider church with a constant inflow of new practices and ideas, and at the same time was protected from the constant temptation to reinvent the Gospel in new ways. The Benedictines' submission to the church did not result in their being submerged in the much laxer practices of the wider church; it instead resulted in the wider church being transformed by the example and teaching of the monastic communities.

III. Stories of New Monasticism in the Church

The Sixties

The Civil Rights Movement, the anti-Vietnam War Movement, and the Cultural Revolution of the 1960s were together an experience that those of us who lived through it will never forget, but still do not understand. But we are now far enough from it to see at least some of its impact. On the one hand it has made racial equality and gender equality part of the social consensus—although we have far to go in achieving these goals. But on the other hand it has embedded a deep individualism in American culture that has in effect legitimized any behavior that can be described as involving consenting adults.

The result is a Culture War that dominates our political and religious life. This war involves issues such as abortion and homosexuality, but behind these battles there is a more fundamental question: to what extent are individuals free to do anything they choose, and to what extent are they responsible for the moral structures of their society? In the Sixties we were so intent on changing society that we never bothered to ask what would happen when these vast changes took place. We now know that the answer is a plague of drug use, sexual promiscuity and divorce. Had we listened to church history, we could have seen that.

Lack of concern for the structures of society is a temptation that any group of idealistic reformers will face. That is why it is so important once again to stay closely connected to the churches. Some people will be friendly to our cause; others will be hostile; still others will consider us deluded. But from all these persons, hostile and friendly, we have something to learn, and all of them can help us understand the impact our efforts are having on the church and society. At the heart of the Great Tradition there is the concept of the common good. That concept is the only real alternative to individualism, and if we are to replace the current tide of destructive individualism with a truly Christian alternative, we will need to listen to the church—all the church.

Reba Place Fellowship

This intentional community was founded in the mid-50s by faculty and students at the Mennonite seminary and college in Goshen, Indiana and grew directly out of the American Mennonite Church experience. Although the initial group realized they were called to something different than the average Mennonite congregation of the time, they still felt it was important to be connected to the Mennonite Church.

In the beginning the Mennonite Voluntary Service program seemed to offer the best link to the Mennonite Church. In the VS program Mennonite youth lived in community, received only room and board, and devoted themselves to Christian service for a period of two years. The founders of Reba Place felt called to do this on a lifetime basis, so they formed an official link with Mennonite Central Committee and began a unit in Evanston, Illinois in 1957.

At the same time, they made it clear they were called to be more than a VS unit—that is, they wanted to become a local congregation. This was shared with leaders of the Illinois Mennonite Conference who recognized the founding group of Reba Place as a potential church plant. This connected with a desire in the conference to establish some kind of pastoral ministry for the 100 Mennonite young men who were then working at Evanston Hospital to fulfill their alternative service obligation to the US government.

These two connections structured a deliberate and positive relationship between the larger church and the new group forming in Evanston, but at the same time the relationship was clouded by considerable suspicion and distrust in the Mennonite Church at large, and by considerable self-righteousness and lack of respect within the Reba group. As a result neither connection lasted. The Reba Place group evolved away from its original VS unit identity, and at the same time there was growing divergence between the congregational expectations of the young men at Evanston Hospital and the growing intentional community at Reba Place. Eventually a peaceful separation was arranged and two separate congregations emerged.

This left Reba Place Fellowship without formal connection to the Mennonite Church, and for the next 12-15 years Reba continued as an unaffiliated renewal community with a significant but only informal connection to the Mennonite Church.

This changed in the early 1970s when Reba experienced a renewal of spiritual and community life under the impact of the Charismatic renewal. Considerable leadership for this came from the Episcopal Church of the Redeemer in Houston, Texas. Out of a sense of submission to Graham Pulkingham, the leader of the Houston group, Reba decided to re-open the question of denominational affiliation. His counsel strongly favored such an alignment, rooted in their renewal experience in Houston which proceeded under a clear sense of submission to the Episcopal bishop in that diocese.

As members of Reba Place prayed about how and where to connect, it seemed clear that they should seek connection with both the Mennonite Church and the Church of the Brethren, since persons from both denominations were an important part of the Reba community. Connecting with both seemed like a way to express an ecumenical vision that went beyond denominational-ism—something that has always been important at Reba. Fortunately, there was sufficient mutual respect that their request for membership was warmly received in both denominations. There was no attempt to diminish or redefine the uniqueness of Reba to fit a denominational pattern.

While some of the original self-righteousness and sense of spiritual superiority certainly continued at Reba, this had been tempered a lot by prolonged experience and by the work of God in members' hearts. Establishing a formal connection with the larger body of Christ opened the door for significant relationship and sharing, which has flowed both ways over the years: the denominations contributed to Reba, and Reba contributed to the denominations. The extent of this exchange was much greater than would have been possible without a membership connection.

Within the last few years, Reba Place has come to see that staying connected with two denominations required going to more denominational meetings than seemed right or possible. They have therefore withdrawn membership from the Church of the Brethren and continued only with the Mennonite Church.

Bridgefolk

In the Bridgefolk movement of which I am a part, the effort to be accountable to the churches to which we belong is central. On the one hand we are a grassroots movement which had its beginnings in the convictions and efforts of a few individuals. At the same time, we can only achieve our goal by forging meaningful relationships with the leadership of both the Mennonite Churches and the Roman Catholic Church.

At first this seemed so impossible that we could only dream of success at some distant date in the future. But we moved ahead in faith anyway, beginning with the relationships we already had, nurturing them, and constantly asking for counsel and support. We tried to make it clear that our goal is to serve the church, not to make additional difficulties for it. We did not take an adversarial position to any other group in the church, and we did not criticize persons we disagreed with. We bent over backward trying to be positive in our outlook and in our actions.

The result has been beyond our wildest dreams. People in both the Mennonite and Catholic communities that we would never have thought would be interested in our effort have come to join us. Although we have proposed something that is utterly new and unprecedented for both Mennonites and Catholics—a space where persons can authentically participate in both communities—we have received very little criticism and very large amounts of support. When we first began we expected some vigorous controversy, but that has not taken place. We all too often underestimate the church. I certainly did in this case. I underestimated our potential for unity and the support for our efforts on the leadership level in both communities. That is surely a hopeful sign of the Holy Spirit's work.

Communities of intentional Christians which have established strong and accountable relationships with the wider church have survived and lived out their original visions. There are many ways to structure accountable relationships with the church. What matters is not which one we choose, but that we choose one of the options available to us and put it into practice, regardless of the difficulties. The alternative is to act as though we are the only Christians who have ever lived.

Mark 6: Intentional Formation in the Way of Christ and the Rule of the Community Along the Lines of the Old Novitiate

David Janzen

I. Treasures Old and New

"I'm a renegade monk," is how my friend and Reba neighbor, Tom Roddy, describes himself. Fifty years ago, before Vatican II, Tom was a novice in the Maryknoll order, preparing to be a missionary priest. Since I have no personal experience of traditional monasticism, I asked Tom to tell me about "the old novitiate."

"I joined Maryknoll at the age of nineteen," Tom continued, "right after high school. To become a priest you did four years of seminary, then a year as a novice, and if you professed vows, you had four more years of upper-level theology study before ordination.

"The life was highly regimented. From day one we did an hour of silent prayer each morning before mass and breakfast. Then off to our classes. Except for an hour of recreation after supper, there was essentially no conversation. We cultivated a climate of monastic silence. We treasured silence and learned to listen carefully when someone had something to say. I thought it was healthy. Silent prayer was a treasured part of my spiritual formation.

"The novice year in Maryknoll was with about sixty-five other young men in Bedford, Massachusetts. We had no course of study. The life was designed to develop self-knowledge and a habit of personal prayer. We put in four hours a day at manual labor. A colleague and I were responsible for the care and feeding of 3,000 chickens. I also worked in the bakery. We had time to read our own stuff. I poured over Charles de Foucault and other writings from the Little Brothers of Jesus. We had weekly lectures by the novice master and an hour with a personal spiritual director. 'Reformation of mores' was the purpose of the novice year—renouncing encumbrances of the old life and practicing the new. I was surrounded by good people. At the end of my novitiate I did not hesitate to take the oath of poverty, chastity and obedience.

"I left the monastic community a little over a year later when I was 'kicked out' because of a manic depressive episode that was regarded as a character flaw in those days, rather than a mental illness caused by a chemical imbalance that, I later learned, can be treated. But I think I might have left anyway. I was becoming convinced that society did not need more celibate priests, but more 'Christians' in a family life.

"Eventually the Lord put in my way a widow with six children and some years at Reba with people whose spiritual lives I admire. At my age the richest satisfaction is seeing my nine kids leading healthy lives. I still practice an hour of silent prayer every day and immensely enjoy spiritual reading. It strengthens my capacity for faith, hope and love. To be holy is to become more thoroughly oneself. I guess I'll always be a monk of sorts."

Renewal movements have a historical ministry, to preserve in a new setting what has been tested and proven of worth. Jesus said, "Every scribe who has been trained for the kingdom of heaven is like the master of a household who brings out of his treasure what is new and what is old" (Matthew 13:52).

The young upstarts of the new monasticism have asked me to be a "scribe." I represent Reba Place Fellowship, an intentional community that has, in their eyes, persisted a long time in an urban setting through many mistakes and glimpses of glory since its founding in 1957. I think I was also asked to contribute to this book because, as coordinator of the Shalom Mission Communities, I have been privileged to visit a variety of Christian intentional communities over the past decade, paying special attention to their ways of preparing new members for communal life and ministry.

Currently, the greatest joy of my work at Reba is engaging with six young interns who are pressing me to learn and share all I can about discipleship, community and service. Our core curriculum has been the Gospel of Luke as we examine how Jesus engaged with his disciples to form them into the Messianic community. What I'm writing here reflects an ardent hope the Holy Spirit is giving us that God is forming many young people for a new generation of prophetic Christian community.

So, if we are looking for resources to support and guide the formation of novices (i.e. new members) for Christian community, it is useful to look at the "old novitiate." But in so doing we may not be thinking "old" enough. We should begin with a novitiate almost 2,000 years old. Forming new members for Christian community is essentially fulfilling Jesus' commission to "go and make disciples of all nations." We "make disciples" by passing on in a contemporary manner the formation that the first disciples received from Jesus.

II. *The Novitiate in Scripture and Tradition*

Generation One—It is the Father's good pleasure to give you the kingdom

For three years Jesus shared an intimate life with his disciples. There was some formal instruction, but most of Jesus' teaching, according to the Gospels, took place "on the road." Whatever happened—healings, confrontations with authorities, scandalous pronouncements of forgiveness, conflicts among the disciples, the power of prayer manifest in their master's life—all became teachable moments. Jesus' main concern seemed to be to help the disciples "see" the Kingdom of God as a present and in-breaking reality, and seeing it, to locate their lives in an adventure of living together, now, this future that God intends for the whole world. "It is the Father's good pleasure to give you the kingdom."

In order to make room in their lives for Jesus' new society, the invitation was necessarily linked to renunciation of the world as they had known it and their attachments to it. It is an instructive exercise to scan the Gospels and note all the renunciations that Jesus asks of his disciples. These renunciations include, but are not limited to, personal possessions, oaths and idle talk, the right to have enemies, worry, making judgments of people God has forgiven, careers, and family expectations. This list, partial as it is, seems like the heroic stuff of super-Christians. But Jesus assumed these renunciations came at the beginning of the life of discipleship. How often we read, "You cannot be my disciple unless you..."

Renunciation itself is not holiness, but it creates a necessary space where the holiness of God can dwell and can reorder the disciples' lives. Some of these renunciations, like family and career, happened just by leaving everything and following Jesus. Others, like renouncing personal possessions and judgments, came with the shared life of Jesus and his camp followers. Renunciation became real as disciples were trained and practiced new virtues in the company of believers. Other renunciations might be lifelong struggles. But if seekers did not want to make these renunciations, they went home, back to the life they used to live.

But the attraction of the Father's love in Jesus, drawing the disciples into his fellowship, made the renunciations of competing attachments seem like part of the good news. In an itinerant fellowship the disciples were urged to "hear and do" what Jesus taught in order to lay a solid foundation for community and ministry. And when the Lord sent them out, it was two-by-two so that the good news would be not just words, but a social reality in which others could see the mutual submission of the Kingdom enacted.

Finally, the divine authority of Jesus to ask his disciples to "love one another as I have loved you" was proven in his own death and resurrection. Moments of intimate fellowship with the risen Lord pointed the disciples away from depending on his physical presence toward a dependence on the promised Holy Spirit.

Generation two—the Apostles prepares new believers in the Spirit's power

The tongues of fire that fell on the believers' heads at Pentecost recall the baptism of Jesus and the voice he heard from heaven. Empowered by the same Spirit, the apostles began a new cycle of disciple-making in the church at Jerusalem, this time on the scale of five thousand newly-baptized believers.

For several years they lived together in the love that wants to share all, available for training into a new way of life and community. They listened daily to the apostles' teaching, learned a radical manner of hospitality within their new extended family, sold off capital assets to care for the needy, and worked out creative ways to distribute the goods of community so that none would be overlooked.

Generation three—to the ends of the earth

When persecution scattered the Jerusalem church, a third cycle of discipleship formation ensued in Antioch and around the Mediterranean. The same Spirit-empowered renunciation of ownership and dedication to the needs of the saints followed. Family-style sharing broke through with all who joined the "Way," whatever their class, race or culture. The Gospels preserve the ways in which Jesus' teachings, parables and actions were remembered and passed on to those preparing to join the community of believers. Biblical scholars now see the Sermon on the Mount (Matthew 5-7) and the more radical Sermon on the Plain (Luke 6:20-49) as "a prime example of the early catechism, the instruction given to converts at the point of their entrance into the Christian church."[1]

---

[1] John Miller, *The Christian Way* (Scottdale, PA: Herald Press, 1961) pp. 4-5.

By the fourth century, the ardent fire of renewal had cooled off. The faith that once was pacifist and persecuted, now identified the Kingdom of God with the Empire and persecuted its enemies with the sword. The legacy of creedal controversies and doctrinal battles with various heresies had the result that the main form of church membership preparation now was a catechism that focused on right belief and doctrine rather than a life that resembled Jesus with his disciples. Sermon on the Mount Christianity was increasingly hard to find in Christendom.

Voices in the wilderness

Meanwhile, in Egypt, a young man, Anthony, heard the lectionary reading in church, "Go, sell all you have and give to the poor. Then come and follow me." Simply and directly, he did what he thought it said. In the wilderness Anthony allowed himself to be disciplined by the Spirit to do battle against the powers of darkness. Within his lifetime, Anthony's example more than his word, was used by the Spirit to lead thousands of other spiritual-athletes-in-training to join him in scattered desert communities of disciples.

In other parts of the crumbling Roman Empire men and women who wanted to live the life of Jesus with his disciples came together in a variety of hermitic and monastic communities. Benedict of Nursia gathered the best wisdom of these early monastic experiments, and his own experience of community leadership, into a rule of life that for fifteen centuries has proven amazingly balanced, sustainable, and inspiring. Praying the psalms in unison and manual labor were the focal practices of the life together that formed its members in the character of Christ.

III. Practices for a New Monasticism

Every generation of Christian community must be built with treasures preserved from the witness of earlier saints and from new resources that the Holy Spirit is forging in the fiery context of present experience. In this section, I want to take what Benedict has to say about the novices' preparation for membership as an outline for further reflections on suitable building materials, both old and new, for prophetic communities under construction in the 21st century. We begin with some surprisingly inhospitable words that Benedict has to say about visitors to the monastic community:

Test the spirits

Do not grant newcomers to the monastic life an easy entry, but as the apostle says, "Test the spirits to see if they are from God." Therefore, if someone comes and keeps knocking at the door, and if at the end of four or five days has shown patience in bearing harsh treatment and difficulty of entry, and has persisted in the request, then that one should be allowed to enter and stay in the guest quarters for a few days. After that, the person should live in the novitiate, where the novices study, eat, and sleep.[2]

I doubt that present-day intentional Christian communities will want to live in a house where the doorbell rings for five days straight. More likely, the first contact with community seekers will be through a web site or in a youth-group urban immersion work day. Several times a year, at Reba, we host a busload of college students who have come to survey "the church in the city." We take them on a walking tour of our neighborhood, telling stories of God's redemption over the years in our life together. They hear about shared cars, a housing management business that sets rents at the level of costs, a "manna" garage where free food is set out twice a week for whoever comes, a workshop where people check out tools and return them with no supervision, a household where people with various disabilities care for one another in love, the office where earners turn in paychecks so all can live on the same level of care. Some people hear these

---

[2] This and subsequent quotes from the Rule of Benedict come from Joan Chittister, *The Rule of Benedict: Insights for the Ages* (New York: Crossroads Publishing Company, 1993), pp. 151-153.

stories and exclaim, "Wow, I didn't know it was possible for city people to live in our day like the church in Acts 2." A few weeks later we might get a letter saying, "I think God wants me to live with you. Is that possible?" Others hear the same stories, yawn and head back to the bus.

Each community needs to develop processes by which seekers are granted brief visits before an invitation comes to share the life more fully. No web site, pamphlet, or orientation session can let a seeker know what a few days of shared life will tell them about God's call and how it becomes real with very human beings. The basic discernment that seekers face at Reba is not whether they agree with us about theories of community, but whether we agree that God has called them to share their days with us for a time, or for a life.

The Simple Way in Philadelphia has found it useful to describe the way into community commitment by means of an "Onion." These are the layers of the onion moving from the outer to the innermost core: Visitors, Guests, Nomads and Novices, Partners. Visitors come for a brief stay. Guests are invited to stay longer and begin seeking with the community how God might be calling them. Nomads stay for an agreed upon period in order to learn and return to another community. Novices are testing their calling to membership. Partners have made vows to make long-term decisions together and seek God for the community's ongoing vision. The Onion's layers do not necessarily represent increasing maturity. Rather, each layer has "different commitments, expectations, and accountability." It takes time to experience each layer before the seeker can know if this is God's calling.

Recently a Reba intern said he did not want to be called an intern any longer. "I feel like I belong here. I am part of the operation." Recalling the Onion's layers I asked, "Does that make you a nomad or a novice?" His eyes lit up with sudden revelation and he announced decisively, "I'm a Nomavice." As Benedict says, "Tests the spirits to see if they are of God."

The spiritual life is not a few new disciplines added to our ordinary existence like another consumer product. Spirituality is how all of life is ordered from the center where God dwells. For most novices a profound transformation is taking place, which Jesus likened to a seed sprouting underground, a field that grows overnight, unobserved. Jesus' images are organic rather than construction-based. They reflect how it is possible for someone to wake up one morning and be at peace with a life committed to following Jesus with these brothers and sisters, come what may.

The novitiate moves us from one world to another. The world as it is, is not our home. We are created for residence in the Kingdom of God. Of course, this new society is not going to be very attractive for those whose hopes are set on success in the present order. But it will fill with longing those for whom this present world is not working, those left behind by globalization, those stuck in the burned out places in the empire, those who have tasted success in the world and found it empty of meaning.

We do not need to argue whether this life of radical discipleship in community is compulsory for all Christians. There are many justifications for this way of sharing (*koinonia*) in the New Testament. But persons so inclined can find countless arguments to wipe away or resist those "musts" and "oughts" of Jesus. Of all the people I know in community, no one has joined because someone convinced them that they "have to" according to some external rule. Rather, the possibility of Christian intentional community is good news to those who have been moved by the Spirit to want to live as fully as possible the way of Jesus with community support. It is, finally, a privilege extended to those with "ears to hear" and who are impelled by the Spirit to do what they have heard.

Spiritual direction

The role of a "senior chosen for skill in winning souls" is crucial to the novitiate as outlined by Benedict's Rule:

A senior chosen for skill in winning souls should be appointed to look after the newcomer with careful attention. The concern must be whether the novice truly seeks God and shows eagerness for the Opus Dei [i.e. "the work of God" which includes the communal prayers], for obedience and for trials. The novices should be clearly told all the hardships and difficulties that will lead to God. If they promise perseverance in stability, then after two months have elapsed, let this rule be read straight through to them, and let them be told, "This is the law under which you are choosing to serve. If you can keep it, come in. If not, feel free to leave."

Each community should carefully choose the person or persons who can spiritually accompany novices. This person will need the gifts of accurate and empathetic listening, be centered in prayer, and know how to call on other resources within and beyond the community. In some ways this role of novice guide is even more critical now than in the time of Benedict because young people in our day are more likely to come from broken families. They often carry wounds from failed relationships that create a longing for community, but also bring significant defenses and healing agendas.

In our heterogeneous society, young people come with their own worlds of ideas and experiences, from various subcultures that have formed their centers of meaning. Spiritual formation will involve extensive conversation—not to persuade or convince them, but to accompany them as the Spirit helps them sort out their authentic experiences of God and the false paths they have taken.

As in the time of Benedict, the novice experience should be anchored in daily work that is challenging enough to cause growth, but that leaves time for contemplation, self-examination, study, and conversation with other community members who keep asking the novices what God is showing them. Stability of relationships is key, as Benedict points out, because community surfaces the contradictions of our lives. Will we stay, listen, learn and resolve conflicts, or will we flee according to the macho maxim, "When the going gets tough, the tough get going"?

The community's rule

It is inevitable that the novice year will involve crises. They may result in objections to parts of the community's rule. It is important that these conflicts come up before making the membership vows.

If they stand firm, they are to be taken back to the novitiate, and again thoroughly tested in all patience. After six months have passed, the rule is to be read to them, so that they may know what they are entering. If once more they stand firm, let four months go by, and then read this rule to them again. If after due reflection they promise to observe everything and to obey every command given them, let them then be received into the community. . . .

Why is it important for a community to have a rule? Is it not enough to have the Gospels? St. Francis thought so. He thought Jesus' instructions to the disciples sent out in mission, two by two, was a sufficient rule for the Franciscans. But for women who wanted to follow Jesus, he proposed a rule of life. And for those who were already married and with families, he was persuaded to make another rule for what came to be known as the Third Order of St. Francis.

Christian intentional communities have many names for their foundation statement— rule, covenant, commitments, oath, vows. Whatever the name, this document reflects the unity that was given by the Spirit at the time of the community's birth. For the Children of Israel this event was the flight from Egypt and the gift of the Law at Mt. Sinai. Every spiritual descendant who celebrates the Seder meal claims this heritage as if "we were there" and "this happened to us." Likewise for Christians, the bread and the wine of communion do not just remember Jesus' last supper with his disciples then, but we are there ourselves, we betrayed our Lord, and we, too, are forgiven by the offering of his body and blood.

In a similar way, it is important for novice members of Christian communities to own the foundation of their common life and to immerse themselves in this story until it becomes their own. Anniversary celebrations and other enactments of the community history allow novices to put down roots. If this does not happen, then the founding members will be "in the know" with a sense of ownership while later members feel like "second class citizens."

The community rule or covenant statement, no matter how many pages long, is only an outline of the issues that need to be addressed by the novice member. When there is a rub, *that* is the time for conversation with community members or the Spiritual Director. Sometimes the questions of novices bring a fundamental challenge to the faithfulness of the community. This can be healthy, too, although the challenge also needs to be sponsored by the Spiritual Director if it is to be taken seriously.

Most communities update their covenants from time to time as a new generation wants to claim the vision. Or, for the more established orders, each generation writes new commentaries on the original rule.[3]

"Everyone then who hears these words of mine and acts on them will be like a wise man who built his house on a rock" (Matthew 7:24). I think we have been spared many fruitless theological debates at Reba by focusing with our novices on "hearing and doing" the words of Jesus. We come from many different theological traditions and could find much to argue about if we chose to. But our task is simpler—all we have to agree on is what we will do in following Jesus, and on that path the Spirit keeps giving unity. By doing the words of Jesus, new habits of character are formed and traditions of community grow, daring ventures of ministry and witness emerge almost without knowing how it happened.

Celebrating membership

Benedict describes the simple and radical submission to God that is celebrated in membership.

---

[3] I recommend Joan Chittester's *The Rule of Benedict: Insights for the Ages*. A fresh translation is interspersed with her own instructions to readers and the monastic communities under her direction.

When they are to be received, they come before the whole community in the oratory and promise stability, fidelity to the monastic life, and obedience. This is done in the presence of God and the saints to impress on the novices that if they ever act otherwise, they will surely be condemned by the one they mock.

They state their promise in a document drawn up in the name of the saints whose relics are there and of the prioress or abbot, who is present. Novices write out this document themselves, or if they are illiterate, then they ask someone else to write it for them, but put their mark to it and with their own hand lay it on the altar. After they have put it there, the novice begins the verse:"Receive me, O God, as you have promised, and I shall live; do not disappoint me in my hope" [Ps. 119:116]. The whole community repeats the verse three times, and adds the doxology. Then the novices prostrate themselves at the feet of each member to ask prayers, and from that very day they are to be counted as one of the community.

When St. Francis' dear friend, Claire, chose to become the bride of Christ in community with other sisters, her head was shaved. The sixteenth-century Hutterites had a custom in their membership ceremony, whereby the novice would have one last look at all the possessions she or he had brought to community. The material goods were placed on one side of the room, and the community members on the other. One last look—a final choice.

Peter asked Jesus an implied question, "Look, we have left everything and followed you." Jesus answered, "Truly I tell you, there is no one who has left house or brothers or sisters or fields, for my sake and for the sake of the good news, who will not receive a hundredfold now in this age—houses, brothers and sisters, mothers and children, and fields, with persecutions—and in the age to come eternal life. But many who are first will be last, and the last will be first" (Mark 10:28-31).

The novitiate creates a community context for accountability of our lives. This is much more than an attitude change where I get to keep whatever I had before and call it "God's BMW." The reality of community makes discipleship real in a way that individually controlled spirituality remains forever slippery.

In renouncing good things, Jesus' followers get even more good things, not as personal possessions, but in the new economy of "all things in common" as graces to be enjoyed in a way that no one is left out. Renunciation prepares the novice to handle poverty or money, itinerate ministry or households, urban life or farm lands on behalf of the community or the mission, knowing that these things are not one's own, but belong to Jesus.

What about renouncing family? In Jesus' day, families of birth were more likely to make first claims on their children's loyalty and service than in our age. When the Christian community is at the center of our loyalty, shaping our life, then we are able to love our families in healthier and more sustainable ways. Because Jesus put the family of his disciples as his first affiliation, he had a family and a brother to whom he could entrust his mother at the cross. The church community is a place where those without families can find a home.

The value of discovering as for the first time what the church has always known

For many of us in the Christian intentional community movement, we did not enter by way of a formal novitiate. We entered by participating in the birth of a new community. In that process the community "discovered for the first time" many truths that the older communities, the church, have always known. We went through the glorious, messy process of giving birth and being born at the same time. We were both midwives and the baby.

In Newton, Kansas in 1971, my wife Joanne and I were privileged to participate in the birth of New Creation Fellowship. In that birth experience we were given a fierce loyalty and love for one another as God was doing a new thing among us. But we were immensely helped along the way by regular visits from Reba Place Fellowship and other groups who took us under their wings.

At the New Monasticism gathering several communities told their birth stories, how they began sharing goods and forming community in order to care for homeless people in crisis, in order to minister to children of the inner city, in order to protest corporate pollution. The Holy Spirit blessed them; they discovered a kinship with the believers described in Acts 2 who shared "all things in common" to meet the needs. What if the whole church lived this way, they wondered. Hey, let's start a revolution! And then they found out that, indeed, scores of other communities were living a life of radical sharing, sacrificial ministry, prophetic witness. Indeed, there have been faithful communal witnesses to Jesus' radical teachings in every century since Pentecost. The purpose of the New Monasticism gathering was, in fact, to link up communities new and old, and to draw on the counsel of friends.

The disastrous end of certain cultic communities who isolate themselves from the wider church should warn us. When one teaching or one teacher becomes the focus of all a community's zeal, watch out! Our experience is that new communities either fail in a few years, or they become unstable and pernicious if they lack the balance that comes from wider counsel. New communities are more likely to survive and remain healthy if they are the offspring of other communities. But new communities are also a source of Holy Spirit innovation adapting old wisdom to new contexts and challenges.

The Bruderhof has encouraged the formation of a new community, young people ministering the presence of Christ in the rough inner city of Camden, New Jersey. The experiment is underway, and has the potential to change the neighborhood, the communal participants, and the parent communities who sent out these pioneers.

Systematic attention to the novice experience becomes important for a community as it seeks to bring a second generation of members into full discipleship and full partnership. This calls for theological reflection to discern what is essential and what is secondary. The novice year focuses on "hearing and doing" Jesus' words, but how this experience is structured calls for a new level of theological reflection on the part of the community and its leaders that remembers the mistakes and blind alleys of the wider church and its history. This is one reason why Reba Place Fellowship has found it important to affiliate with Shalom Mission Communities, with the Mennonite Church and with other informal Christian contacts that allow us to give and receive counsel.

IV. New Monasticism: Idol or Authentic Work of God

Alasdair MacIntyre's oft-quoted conclusion in *After Virtue*, is that our increasingly fragmented and barbarous Western Civilization can only be saved by a new Benedict. This is the somewhat grandiose idea behind his call for a new monasticism that can produce disciplined communities sustaining the virtues of civilized life.

Such a call for a new monasticism would have sounded idolatrous to Benedict who had no intention of saving "Western Civilization." The hundreds of monastic communities that followed his rule did build up industrious and non-violent communities of refuge in a Europe perpetually at war, preserve literacy in an age that scorned learning, and allow for serious reflection generation after generation on what was good, true and beautiful. But these monastic communities could bear such fruit only because they considered these things worthy of a life's devotion. Their roots were in the worship of God, and their branches were the training of disciples in the way of Jesus. Good fruit would naturally grow from a good tree. The new monasticism, likewise, will have little of value to offer the world if it tries to meet the needs of the world as defined by the world. What the world needs is Jesus, and a people who allow their lives to be radically reshaped in communities demonstrating love and non-violence of the One who sent Jesus.

This essay has focused on the challenge posed by Jesus, to bring out the best treasures of the saints, both old and new, for the task of making disciples. We have commended the following partial list of tested and approved elements of the old novitiate for consideration by new discipleship communities:

- The radical teachings of Jesus, especially those found in Matthew 5-7 and Luke 6;
- Renunciations that move us from individual control of our lives into a communal context, making room for Kingdom of God commitments;
- The gifts of a spiritual director or novice master;
- At least a year of formation in a shared life of work, prayer, and fidelity in reconciled relationships;
- A rule or a covenant that outlines the birth experience and unity of community;
- Celebrations that mark the passage from darkness into the light of a shared life in Christ;
- Connections that give and receive counsel in the wider church and communal movement.

Finally, we affirm our hope. Our hope is not in America, not in Western Civilization, and not in our communities. Our hope is in Jesus and the power of his Spirit at work in communities of faithful discipleship, witnessing to God's nonviolent regime change already breaking into history, inviting all to a place at the banquet of love where all can live at peace.

Mark 7: Nurturing Common Life Among Members of Intentional Community

Sherrie Steiner and Michelle Harper Brix

I. Healing: My Own Story

The largest intentional Christian community I (Sherrie) have been part of consisted of 21 people who ate together, prayed together, and shared expenses. Later a smaller group ministered together in the "snake pit" of Pasadena, California, and worked in the same nonprofit organization. Things could get pretty intense. Learning to pay attention to the way in which God is at work in one's life can be quite exciting, but it can also be overwhelmingly painful. Communicating with humans who can be tangibly seen and heard is hard enough, but learning how to see God at work in the midst of the group is far more difficult. In community, as in every Christian life, there is no substitute for the difficult task of separating what we *want* God to be saying from attempting to discern what God might *actually* be saying. If there is a loving and accepting culture within the community, people seldom leave because of poverty, danger (e.g., drive-by shootings), or differences in eating habits, hygiene standards, or music preferences. People usually leave, in my experience, because they can't handle the emotional pain that surfaces.

Just before the end of apartheid in South Africa, I traveled from Pasadena to Cape Town as part of our efforts as a Christian community in the United States to help end the injustice there. When I was in Cape Town, a minister explained to me the living conditions of the people in his parish as we walked through the township of Khayalitsha. We came to a sandy makeshift graveyard. As far as I could see, there were little crosses with names and ages carved into the wood. The minister told me about a funeral he had conducted the day before. Just as he finished the service, the mother of the deceased child threw herself across the coffin, reaching for her baby with sobs. As he recounted the scene, I was still looking around us at the crosses. The oldest age I could see scrawled on the wooden markers was five years old. That visual image of so many young lives cut short brought to mind a flood of tragic stories that I had experienced in our life with poor and hurting people. Poverty, hunger, political injustice, community despair, gang warfare—I had been surrounded by stories upon stories for over ten years. Those stories felt heavy as I stood in that sandy graveyard. I realized that my spirit had grown fragile.

What put me over the edge was an accident with another ministry called Potter's Clay. Beginning when I was a student at Westmont College, over three hundred students from the school traveled to Ensenada, Mexico during Easter break each year to work with churches and orphanages. Several years after my graduation, our community was invited to return to Potter's Clay to hold the chapel in the mornings. This particular year, just as chapel ended, we learned that a drunk driver had hit a car full of students. Three students were killed and two more were severely injured.

The death and injury of the students left an indelible mark upon my life. I felt somewhat responsible for the accident because of my role in the early years of Potter's Clay. I became emotionally detached, unable to cry and unable to care. I had already seen too much in my own life, in my community, and around the world. Now the greatest pain of all came from my efforts to make a difference. Innocent suffering is bad enough, but when you feel responsible for causing it, the pain is worse.

Not long after the car accident that killed the students, we moved from "the snake pit" in Pasadena to the Snake River in Washington State. We needed a safe, quiet place where we could heal and regroup, and this was a farming area with extended family. For a few years, as part of our healing, we invited friends to a weeklong Christian art festival held on our farm. While others drew, wrote, painted, and carved statues, I repeatedly did one thing: I would cover a canvass with as many pastel colors as I could find. When it was completely covered, I would take a black crayon and draw huge teardrops on top of the pastels. I called these the "Teardrops of God." They signified my prayer to God about my own emotional disconnectedness. Year after year I consistently painted this same theme while others did a variety of artistic expressions. Needless to say, I was "stuck." And yet, each redrawing was a prayer to God.

After three years of this, we were invited to celebrate the twentieth anniversary of Potter's Clay. We went and all the founding members were there. We reminisced, looked through two decades of photos, and thanked God for all that had happened through the years. We were almost finished when one of the students who survived the car accident, Megan, stood up and asked to speak. "I wanted to come speak to you today because I knew that some of you might be wishing you hadn't started Potter's Clay because of what happened with us." She was right. "Well," she said, "I want you to know that it was worth it. And if it was worth it to me, it should be worth it to you."

I was stunned. The last time I had heard about her she was nearly dead. Yet, here she was, standing and quite lucid. She told us about her amazing recovery that had surprised all of the doctors. Then she told us that the closest she had ever felt to God in her entire life was when she was in the coma and when she first returned to the scene of the car accident. "God has never been so real and wonderful in all of my life. Thank you, for starting Potter's Clay."

Megan sat down, and we disbanded shortly afterward. I caught her on the lawn just as she was leaving and asked if I could speak to her just a little more. She stopped and looked at me. Megan recognized who I was and sensed that I was waiting. "There is one thing more," she said. "When I was in the coma, I saw the teardrops of God. I didn't actually see God's face, but I saw God's tears. And the colors of the rainbow were reflected in the tears."

Megan left, but I kept repeating her words over to myself. I felt free for the first time in years. I realized that I had been suffering under an emotional perfectionism—expecting my heart to carry what only God could carry. God wanted me to participate in bringing in the kingdom of God, but it was *God's* responsibility to make it happen, not mine. God had seen my pictures and had heard my prayers. And God used one of the people whose suffering had crushed me to be the messenger of my liberation. God was speaking my language. I had been at the end of my abilities, but God broke into my life with a healing experience. God spoke to me through Megan, and for the first time in a long time, I began to cry. Through Megan I learned that the key to nurturing intentional community is understanding that the origin of human healing is in the Godhead, not in humans.

II. Biblical & Theological Resources for Life Together

If Christians are going to nurture common life among members of intentional community, they must become self-aware enough to know who they are, what they are about and why they are about it. Only then can they be members of a collective that has enough in common to remain united when the mundane realities of living together in a difficult world threaten to tear them apart. From the beginning, Christian community has been influenced by the Hebrew understanding that the people of God, as announced by the Prophets, has a God-given destiny to fulfill. God's people are chosen for a purpose—they are blessed to be a blessing to *all* the nations (e.g., Gen. 22:15-18; Psalm 105). In the New Testament, the teachings of Jesus centered on the kingdom of God (e.g., Mt. 13:24, 13:31, 13:33, 13:44, 13:45; Lk 10:9, 12:31) that the Messiah would usher in. Unlike many religions that sought salvation through escape from social reality, Christian community sought salvation through ethical engagement in both time and history out of obedience to the will of God (e.g., Mt. 25:36-46; James 2:14-25). Early Christian spirituality was future-oriented and hope-filled despite opposition and outright persecution. Early Christian communities were not enslaved to a future that was determined by the past. Rather, they were free to redefine the bounds of hope as embodied in their collective response to the life of Christ. As John Zizioulas has written:

> The decisive battle against the powers of evil had been won and the final destiny of the world, a destiny of un-ceasing and abundant life (John 2:10), of light (Matt 4:16), of justice (2 Pet. 3:13), and of joy (Luke 2:10) had been granted to humanity and the entire creation in the person of the risen Christ. Humanity's relation with God is, there-fore, marked by the celebration of this victory over the powers of evil and death.[1]

The German New Testament scholar Oscar Cullman likened this to the way in which D-Day was the decisive battle that sealed the victory of the Allied forces during World War II, even though more soldiers died *after* this turning point than during all the time prior. Christ-centered Christianity enabled early Christians to re-main ethically engaged with social struggles because they knew that, whether they succeeded or failed, they were part of a larger Christian history that would ultimately be victorious. The main battle had already been won through the birth, death and resur-rection of Jesus Christ. So, for the early Christians, common life in intentional communities revolved around Christian obedience to the will of God. While natural affections would be nurtured, those affections would *not* be the path to the new creation. Christians

---

[1] For this historical information I am drawing on John Zizioulas essay "The Early Christian Community," in *Christian Spirituality: Origins to the Twelfth Century*, Volume 16 of *World Spirituality: An Encyclopedic History of the Religious Quest*.

were taught to become the initiators of loving behavior in human social relations out of gratitude for what God had done for them. Eventually, the Messiah would come again and fulfill the "eschatological salvation."

In the meantime Christian community became characterized by *longing*, a manifestation of the tension between the "now" and the "not yet." The paradox of Christians living between history and eschatology was nurtured in community as they shared meals in communion with God and one another as a form of presence, while at the same time praying for justice, patience, endurance, and other gifts of the Holy Spirit in expectation of Christ's return. Strong maintenance of this longing became a force of decisive importance for Christian community because it was the longing that shaped the spirituality of the early Christians.

Early Christian communities worshiped Jesus the Christ who they knew to be preparing the way for them, cheering for their endurance, advocating on their behalf and offering them the assurance that they would be favorably received and answered by God. The community became the sign of the coming kingdom to people searching for God—a place that modeled a 'way of being' that overcame all divisions, both natural and social, in the transcendent unity celebrated in the Eucharist. An enduring pattern emerged where *longing* gathered the Christians together (I Cor. 11:20), united them in communion (Gal. 3:28), and then sent them out to minister in the community (Matt. 28:18-20). These three characteristics eventually became marks of the Eucharistic community in the early church.

But this longing is also vulnerable to distortion. Communities need a daily sense of direction. While it is true that monastic movements grow when they are able to formulate a Christian response to needs at a particular moment in history, sustaining a common life requires spontaneously directed negotiation of daily twists and turns that can make or break a community. This latter point is what makes this seventh mark much more difficult than it may seem at first. One way, although certainly not the only way, to make nurturing decisions that heal and stimulate growth is to identify particular pitfalls to avoid as communities journey toward the kingdom of God.

In what follows I will name five ways our longing for the kingdom can fall victim to distortion by giving way to obsession, desire, ecstasy, detachment, and despair.

Obsession: Longing becomes obsession when we behave as if our salvation depends upon us ushering in the kingdom of God here and now. There is a desperation that undermines the gospel when we behave as if participation in the kingdom of God is our path to heaven rather than a foretaste of heaven. The gospel teaches that we are not capable of earning our way to heaven. When we begin to participate in the kingdom of God with a command and control spirit, our behavior loses its ethical character and we have begun to sidestep obedience as the pathway to heaven.

Desire: When we become *takers* from God and others instead of *givers* as God instructs, longing has given way to unbridled desire. Perhaps we think we deserve better after all we have done. Perhaps we cease to care about salvation and become concerned only with immediate pleasure and pain. Perhaps we commit what Old Testament scholar John Bright calls Israel's fatal mistake in the Old Testament—confusing God's favor with favoritism and ceasing to take seriously the command to practice justice and hospitality. Scripture teaches that we are blessed to be a blessing to others (e.g., Genesis 15, Matt. 28:18-20). When Jesus got angry in the temple, it was because the people had taken an area that was supposed to be a place of *prayer for* all the nations and made it, instead, into a *marketplace of economic exploitation* (Isaiah 56:6-8, Matt. 21:12-13).

We live in a society that will inevitably affect us. Capitalism requires a certain amount of narcissism to function well, but that is no excuse for us Christians to keep ourselves the center of attention when Scripture teaches us to care for others (e.g., Isaiah 58, James 1:19-27). Manipulating other people as objects to be used for our own pleasure is dehumanizing. Similarly, praying to

God only to get what we want in particular circumstances is more like practicing magic than relating spiritually to God.

Ecstasy: The new monasticism is located in what has increasingly become a culture of eroticism in the United States—an ethos of love for love's sake. It should come as no surprise, then, that the new monasticism will likely be affected by this culture to develop an intimate ecstasy model with God. While the intimate/ecstasy relationship has been shown to be emotionally renewing, and human sexuality can be holy and positively transforming, ecstasy as a trancelike, self-obliterating experience of 'visitation from the Living God' cannot bring salvation. God cannot be reduced to human projections.

God incarnate entered history to transform it. God calls us to do the same. The origin of human healing is in the Godhead, not the human situation. This is critical because if our salvation depends upon humans embedded in systems of sin, we are no longer saved from ourselves by the grace of God. In divinizing human sexuality we blind ourselves from God's act of deliverance for the whole world.

The new monasticism must take care to put faith in the gospel instead of the transcendence that is possible between humans. We love because God first loved us as actualized in the incarnation and the church. To the extent that lay communities exist in human homes, the relationship of these communities with the institutional church is a test case for this issue. According to Athanasian spirituality, the church forms the believing community into a liturgical, institutional, and theological celebration of the divine incarnation. As Ivan displayed in chapter five, the institutional church offers the new monasticism a reference point—a place of mooring—for always remembering the good news that God has saved us from ourselves.

Detachment: Ascetic emotional control is essential to a methodical way of life in monastic communities. Too much detachment has its associated dangers, however. For the Gnostics, religious history became displaced by religious analogy and systematization. Ultimately left with only a pessimistic dualism, they eventually died out as a movement.

The Gnostics tried a variety of means to reclaim divine emotions and thus bridge the gap between the divine and the human, but all of them ultimately distanced God from the world and rejected God's divine involvement in history. Members of the new monasticism may find themselves tempted to, like the Gnostics, substitute knowledge *about* God for the direct relationship *with* God as a means of redemption. Gnostics were known for their claim that salvation came through "secret knowledge"—ritualistic understandings that were simply the opposite of ignorance. Like Gnosticism, monasticism values learning and ritual. But Christians practice asceticism for very different reasons than Gnostics. For Christians, God entered history, took responsibility for what He created, and saved humans from themselves. Knowing God is not the same as knowing about God.

Despair: The asceticism of monastic living has been known to cause religious melancholia. The demands of living emotionally detached has periodically engendered a sense of personal crisis that a continued pursuit of the calling could not assuage. Max Weber was aware of these depressive side-effects, but he thought the psychic costs associated with the "ceaseless striving to make a life devoted to ultimate values and ethical responsibility" was justifiable. The notion of spiritual pilgrimage as equivalent to consistent living before God has a downside where people experience religious "failure" and experience feeling forsaken by God. What distinguishes a Christian response from Gnosticism is that faith is introduced as the critical element in community renewal. Christianity affirms life and the goodness of creation, but the new creation *emerges from* faith—it is *not* the path toward faith.

In each of the cases above, the Christian attempts to escape from the tension that comes with living between the now and the not yet. With obsession, the Christian consumes or is consumed by her "spirituality." With misguided desire, the Christian becomes self-centered and makes God into an object to be manipulated. With ecstasy, the Christian and God form a couplet that narcissistically shuts out the rest of the world. With detachment and despair, the Christian disengages from the interpersonal bond with God.

Communities of the new monasticism must structure their common life in such a way that enables members to experience their longing for the kingdom rightly, free from the destructive distortions of the world. At best, neo-monastic communities may provide a space where Christians can taste the eschatological hope of salvation and demonstrate to one another how our longing can witness to God's healing grace at work in our midst.

III. Experiments in Common Life
(These stories by Michelle Harper Brix)

I came to community with a group of college students who, at the time, could not define "intentional community," but we knew in our hearts and minds that the way we had always been told to do life was not what we were looking for. We didn't know exactly what we were seeking, but we knew that climbing the corporate ladder to better ourselves at the expense of others seemed quite the opposite of how we had come to understand the gospel of Jesus.

In the autumn months of 1997, six people—some friends, some merely acquaintances—got together over the course of a semester in coffee shops, dorm rooms, lounges, vans, and parks to discuss, in four-hour long meetings four times per week, all the reasons why we felt that living together with shared goals and interests was important. We wanted to "Love God, Love People, and Follow Jesus," (I won't even tell you how long it took us to narrow that down!) and knew that in order to do that, we had to do it together. Our conversations were based around a common experience earlier that year of loving and receiving love from people who were "poor and homeless." As they had become our friends, we fought for their rights to housing, childcare, healthcare, education and living wage jobs, sometimes risking arrest. All six of us had come to the understanding that we could not continue to live outside of the struggles on a posh college campus, but none of us had the street smarts or confidence to move to the inner-city of Kensington on our own. Thus, we began to talk about doing something we truly believed was radical and new, rarely practiced outside of monasteries and convents, and almost unheard of in mainstream American culture: *living together in community.*

We got this "new and radical" concept of a lifestyle from the early church example that was written about in Acts chapters 2 and 4, where the believers lived together and shared everything in common. The only other community we knew of, Jesus People USA in their "Friendly Towers" in Chicago, provided the sole experience we pulled from for our conversations. Because they were hundreds and we were six, it became difficult to find similarities to build from. But we persevered and talked and talked and planned and talked and speculated and imagined and prayed and eventually found ourselves living together in North Philadelphia as The Simple Way Community. Here we have shared our lives together and learned, often the hard way, what it means to be housemates, partners, and community members.

Looking back seven years later, we sometimes laugh at ourselves and our ignorance. How could we have thought ourselves to be resurrecting an ancient and forgotten practice? How could we have missed the rich traditions of Christian community that have survived and thrived throughout the centuries all over the country and the world? Why did we have such a narrow understanding of what intentional Christian community could be? Still, we wouldn't change our history or our journey. It may be that if we had known about all of the other traditions and models of community that our experiment would not have made it for even six months out of fear that somehow we were doing it "wrong." Instead, we built on our longing, our stubbornness to live out the change we dreamed about, and our desire, along with our new neighbors, to see the kingdom of God come on earth as it is in heaven.

Over the seven years that we have existed, The Simple Way

has changed and evolved almost annually, depending on who is in the house and the internal struggles, as well as the needs and struggles of the surrounding neighborhood. We have been as few as five and as many as fourteen, and we have lived in up to three houses in the neighborhood.

When we first began, we chose to live in a way that was very unstructured. We had a schedule for daily and weekly activities, but we did not create a chore and task list, and almost anyone who wanted to be a part of our lives was welcomed to "come and see." As a result, we had no rituals, no space for journey, and no place for accountability. When we grew from seven to fourteen over the course of three months, the lack of structure and roles became an evident problem. By the end of one year together, we had fallen abruptly back to seven. The phenomenon of not having enough emotional energy to withstand the internal issues that arose within community ultimately led to a breakup between several members. I remember driving to our annual summer retreat in Tennessee that year thinking, "Why are we even doing this? We practically hate each other. If we're honest with each other on this retreat, it will be a disaster. If we aren't honest, there will be no point in even opening our mouths."

We had come to a place where we were worn out from trying to do all that we could for hurting and hungry and addicted neighbors (which sometimes simply served our "need" to feel useful and redeemed rather than eliminate their real problems). We did not have "required hours" to put in as members of the community. Such rules were avoided under the guise of, "If you love me and love other people (and Jesus, ultimately), you'll help me cook for all these hungry people or be willing to run someone off to detox at a moment's notice at 2 a.m." Some members of the community would be hard at work in the house from dawn to dusk while others would merely show up at meetings. This created lots of internal hurt and anger. Some members spread themselves thin while others fostered their lives outside the tasks of The Simple Way. As a result, we avoided one another when we didn't have to work together.

Our retreat ended up being a very hard but somewhat amazing time together. It wasn't all love and hugs, but early on we came to realize that our lack of structure, organization, and clear roles was actually playing a major part in sucking the health out of our ailing community. Out of our talks and meetings in Tennessee, we came up with our "Onion," which David Jansen describes in more detail in chapter six.[2] The Onion created a structure for potential members to journey into the community in a very intentional way without expecting someone who had lived with us for three weeks to be a part of making major decisions about our activities and convictions immediately. It also created space for members to choose how deeply they wished to be committed to the activities and tasks of the community, as well as the other members.

The Onion is not without its glitches and inadequacies, and didn't solve all of our problems. (In fact, seven members still left the community within three months of that retreat. Too much damage had already been done.) But what I find to be most incredible about the Onion is that it was created in a setting where somehow, despite our anger and pain, we were able to grant each other grace and forgiveness. We were able to work out the crux of our issues with one another (in most cases) and deal with those realities rather than harp on pettier incidents or situations. This could not have happened without the willingness of all to share and be vulnerable to the process.

From June 2003 to May 2004, my husband Michael and I decided to have some rest and reflection apart from The Simple Way, where we had spent the entirety of our married lives – five and a half years. We wanted to figure out if this sort of community was what we were "called" to and if The Simple Way was the only place we could live that out. Among other topics, we were also considering starting a family and wanted to explore the idea of children in community together. So we began traveling around the country in a small motor home, visiting friends and family

---

[2] This schematic is also available on our webpage, www.thesimpleway.org.

and other communities we'd met or heard about, sleeping in driveways (and WalMart parking lots), and asking a lot of questions of one another as well as the wise and wonderful folks who hosted us along the way. I will tell you specifically about three places we stayed and their distinct ways of communal living.

Rome City, Indiana: Not a big town. Lots of Amish. A friend of Michael's lives there and invited us into his home to stay as we passed through. The catch was, by the time we got to Rome City, Michael's friend didn't really have a home in which to host us. He and his family had been staying with another family from church while they waited for the sale to close on their new home. But the friends from church were happy to have us as well, and it was a big party! (Of course it was a party; there were four children in the house, all under age four!) When we stayed with these two families, we witnessed community happening. They never would have defined themselves as an intentional community. But there they were, taking care of each other, working on the house together, babysitting each other's kids, sharing meals when they could. They didn't analyze what they were doing or why it was important. They didn't create a mission statement. They simply lived, and took care of each other, not because it was a radical way to live, but because it just made the most sense.

Tacoma, Washington: In Tacoma we visited a L'Arche Community. L'Arche Communities are places where folks who have various degrees of functionality in terms of learning, developmental and physical disabilities live together. Their mission statement says it best: "No matter what the level of our abilities or disabilities, we all share a common humanity. We belong together in the human family. We uphold the dignity of each person by creating relationships where we seek to grow together in mutual respect and love." Michael and I saw this mission upheld in the most sincere and genuine ways. They live, eat, work and share their lives together. This is not a situation where social workers help the clients. They are all in it together, no matter how different they may be from each other. The community, the reciprocity, and the shared support there blew our minds.

Shreveport, Louisiana: Here we found a group of families and individuals living communally but in separate houses; some of them do not even attend the same church. Most of them have children, from toddlers to teenagers and older. Most of them have established careers. Over the past five years, they all have discovered the danger in the pursuit of the "American Dream" and have begun to reconsider what it means to follow Jesus in a world that demands upward mobility and individualism in order to care well for your family. So they call themselves "Common Ground Community." They started working with the sister congregation of their affluent church organizing and serving free meals for kids and families, starting a community garden, and sharing meals and journeys together in this new adventure. They are trying to figure out together how to teach their children a new way to look at life without alienating them. This group of amazing people is such an encouragement to those of us who have been discouraged by people who say that community can only happen when you're young, but must be abandoned when you want to "settle down."

As Michael and I returned from our trip and processed all we had seen and experienced, we came to understand that there are countless ways to consider and define community. There is no one model to follow, and there isn't a wrong way to create a nurturing community as long as people commit themselves to love one another sacrificially just as Christ loves the world. This realization gives me the freedom to discover nurturing forms of community that don't look like The Simple Way.

In the communities of the new monasticism, mainstream churches may find new, hopeful ways the Holy Spirit works to nurture Christians in the faith. And the neo-monastic communities must resist the temptation of prideful, narcissistic sectarianism by entering into conversation with other communities (conventional and non-conventional) and learn how God is moving differently in their midst. Nurturing common life should not turn into navel-gazing. Rather, it is an opportunity to create connections with other communities that serve to edify all parties involved.

Mark 8: Support for Celibate Singles Alongside Monogamous Married Couples and Their Children

Jana Bennett

"If we regulate our households by
seeking the things that please God,
we will also be fit to oversee the Church,
for indeed the household is a little Church."
John Chrysostom, fourth century

I. Celibacy or Marriage?

"Celibacy or marriage?" has been a crucial question as I have wrestled with how best to serve God. My questioning began when I was in college and taking classes from some Carmelite monks[1] who lived a few hours away. Eventually, I spent so much time with them that they asked if I wanted to consider a deeper, more binding relationship with them. I fell in love with them, just as I might have fallen in love with a potential spouse.

---

[1] The Carmelites are a religious group within the Roman Catholic Church who practice contemplative living as hermits for long periods during the year. Following these intense periods of contemplation, they venture into the world, doing service that is representative of the fruits of their contemplation of Christ. The Carmelites have a history that stretches back at least to the twelfth century, but they claim Elijah as their spiritual ancestor.

As monks, these Carmelites took a vow of celibacy. As a Protestant, I was unsure of what celibacy meant. To me it had always seemed like some crazy thing Catholic priests and a few other odd people do. Yet the more time I spent with my Carmelite friends, the more I began to wonder if there wasn't, in fact, something very, very good about the practice of celibacy. For one, I noticed that the male Carmelite monks did not treat me as a sexual object, unlike almost all the men I had encountered at college. The Carmelite men treated me as a person to be respected and as a friend. For another, these monks seemed free and joyful about following God, in a way that I had never before experienced. They loved God and saw that their practice of celibacy was a way of becoming more Christ-like because they were free to love all people.

I had long had questions about whether marriage was in fact good; it seemed that the institution of marriage was falling apart everywhere I looked. My friends were getting divorced and children were being hurt. The wedding industry itself displayed a sickening array of "must-have" objects and traditions (the $10,000 photographer, for instance) that claimed to be the perfect beginning to the perfect marriage (one that wouldn't end in divorce). I found, too, that I wasn't altogether sure what the purpose of marriage was. All my friends seemed to be having sex and getting along just fine without marital commitments from their boyfriends. Women's magazines seemed to suggest that marriage was for good interpersonal relationships, but there again I had to protest. After all, I had several good interpersonal relationships with people that had nothing to do with marriage. My Catholic friends might have heard that the point of marriage was for children, but what I heard was that they were mostly a nice side effect of marriage. So, if marriage wasn't needed for sex or friendship or children, what was the point? Moreover, if marriage's stability was clearly not guaranteed in our society, I wasn't sure I wanted a part of it. Marriage, from my point of view, seemed dead.

So, at the end of my college career, when the monks asked if I wanted to try living with them, I seriously considered it for a couple years. During this discernment period, I began a fairly serious dating relationship with "Adam." This was not considered problematic to my potential involvement with the Carmelites; in fact, most monastic communities these days encourage it. Though "Adam" and I had not yet begun talking about marriage, the seriousness of our relationship caused me to rethink my earlier musings. I began pondering marriage from a Christian theological point of view rather than examining marriage's death in our culture. One of the most important realizations came when I looked at Paul's letter to the Ephesians more thoroughly. Paul suggests that marriage somehow enacts the relationship between Christ and the church.[2] So marriage is vastly important to Christians, not because of its social implications but because it has *theological* significance. Marriage tells us something about God. Those who are married in some way live lives that grow more and more in Christ's life and love for us. I know that this is not always the case in marriage, just as I know that celibacy is not always practiced well. Nonetheless, I saw that marriage might have a more sacred purpose than I had been led to believe.

In the midst of my wrestling with celibacy and marriage, "Adam" asked me to marry him. There I was, suddenly faced with *two* decisions: one for celibacy and one for marriage. I panicked because I couldn't figure out how to choose between the two; I couldn't decide how to know where God was leading me. That was when I realized the grace of the wider Christian community. As I struggled desperately to make the "right" decision that would

---

[2] I do not have space here to deal with all of the exegetical questions surrounding Eph. 5:32. Paul's use here of the word *mysterion*, or "mystery" as it is rendered in English, has caused considerable questions about whether marriage is a mystery alongside Christ and the church, or whether it is *only* the relationship between the church and Christ that is a mystery, while marriage is not. I have chosen to take a higher view of marriage, seeing that it *too* is a mystery, because I think this interpretation is more faithful to the Ephesians letter as a whole. My advice is to examine several Bible commentaries on this matter (e.g. Anchor Bible series, Abingdon, and the like). See also Stephen Miletic, *'One Flesh' – Eph. 5:22-24, 31: Marriage and the New Creation* (Roma :Editrice Pontificio Instituto Biblico,1988).

best let me follow God, I called upon trusted friends who were celibate priests, monks, and lay people, and married or engaged couples. They were the ones who told me about their own experiences and how it was faithfulness to their vows that mattered in the end, not the particular state of life. Though there were differences between the states of life, marriage and celibacy were similar because both entailed vows in the presence of the church. It was not "marriage" *or* "celibacy" that was the main thing, but "marriage" *and* "celibacy" *in the context of the Christian community*. I am glad to say that with the help of this wider community, I decided to make vows with neither the Carmelites nor "Adam" because I was not ready for either one. Instead I began to focus more intently on the practices of Christian communities. It was then that I saw how skewed and problematic our common perceptions of marriage and celibacy had become, especially because these states of life had been largely separated from the church's support.

II. Celibacy and Marriage in Scripture and Tradition

Celibacy or marriage? Both of these "states of life," as they are commonly called in theological circles, represent the two options for living that the church has advocated over the past two thousand years. These are the two states of life for Christians, partly because of Scriptural witness (1 Cor. 7) but also because of the vows involved in both marriage and celibacy. Traditionally, these states of life require resolute, lifelong vows to one person or several people, because living out those vows teaches a person how to love. Scripture and the church's wisdom both claim that love is no mere feeling, nor is it an option simply to be put aside when problems come up. To paraphrase Dorothy Day, vows remind us that as Christians we are not called so much to be successful in our loving as to be faithful to God, whom we know as love. Given the significance of these states of life for Christians, it is necessary for intentional communities to ask, "How are these states of life supported in our community?", "How do we help people discern states of life?" and even more basically, "What do we believe about these two states of life?"

If we spend even a short time looking through the vast material that has been written about either marriage or celibacy, it quickly becomes clear that this has been one of the most confusing and contentious points in Christian history. The common story has been that before the Reformation in the sixteenth century, the Catholic Church overemphasized celibacy (especially in its monastic form) as the more perfect way of life. Augustine, a fifth-century bishop who has been highly influential in subsequent centuries, wrote comparing virginity to marriage: "how much more, and with how much greater honor, are we to reckon among the goods of the soul that continence, whereby the virgin purity of the flesh is vowed, consecrated, and kept, for the Creator Himself of the soul and flesh." Augustine never said that marriage was an evil, as some of his contemporaries did. Nevertheless, he gave celibacy priority. Christians would use his works and those of others to put forth celibate monasticism as the best way to give glory to God. During the Protestant Reformation, reformers such as Martin Luther worked hard to suggest that in fact celibate monasticism was not an appropriate way of life for Christians and that it had been abused. In a letter to three nuns, for example, Luther wrote against celibacy, saying: "Scripture and experience show that among many thousands there is not a one to whom God has given to remain in pure chastity.... Therefore food and drink, sleep and wakefulness have all been created by God. Thus He has also ordered man and woman to be in marital union." From the writings of these two profoundly influential men, then, we can readily see how marriage and celibacy can appear as utterly split from each other.

Thus in contemporary culture both Catholic and Protestant writings have placed far more emphasis on marriage than on celibacy. Often marriage has become a problem to be solved rather than a joy to be celebrated. For example, the Religion, Culture, and Family project at the University of Chicago was begun in an attempt to stem high divorce rates and the problems that marriage has encountered in an age of modernity. Many prominent thinkers have become part of this project, which has written numerous books and essays for both academic and popular audiences.[3] In popular culture, celibacy has become a strange practice to be shunned, especially because of the fallout from the recent clergy sexual abuse scandals. Neither "group" is portrayed as being able to offer any good to the other "group." Throughout Christian history the tendency has been to sharply define and separate marriage and celibacy from each other in ways that have not allowed the church to draw on the gifts and opportunities of each state of life.

The new monasticism has made a decided move against such separation and instead calls for Christian communities to be intentional about supporting each other in both states of life. Both states of life are holy and are supported by scriptural witness as well as the Christian tradition.

We Christians are familiar with "In the beginning, God created" humans as male and female and commanded them to be fruitful and multiply (Gen. 1:22; God speaks similarly to Noah, Gen. 8:17). This theme of "being fruitful" recurs over and over in the Hebrew Scriptures. For example, God's covenant with Abraham included a promise that he would be the father of many (Gen. 17:5). Jacob had twelve sons, whose descendents became the many sons of the tribes of Israel. God promised King David that his lineage would last forever (1 Kings 2:33). These are examples of familiar passages where God's covenant with Israel is directly and physically linked with marriage and children. God's promises here involved offspring, and God promised to work through those offspring.

A related, recurrent theme in Scripture is that of God as the

---

[3] The website for the project is http://divinity.uchicago.edu/family. Many of the publications are listed there. One of the more popular books is *Marriage: Just a Piece of Paper?*, edited by Katherine Anderson, Don Browning, and Brian Boyer (Grand Rapids, MI: Eerdmans Press, 2002). This book contains the transcripts of a PBS documentary by the same title; a video of the documentary is also available.

bridegroom who marries the faithless bride Israel. This theme is poignantly told in the book of Hosea, where the prophet even marries a prostitute as a means of demonstrating, by analogy, God's own extreme faithfulness to us. It is important, then, to be married and to have children, because marriage affirms the fidelity of both God and the couple, and children proclaim to the world that God has bestowed blessings on the couple and the community.

In the Gospel accounts Jesus twists this understanding of marriage a bit. He declares that divorce is to be used in limited ways because of what divorce says about being faithful (Mt. 5:31-32). The parables he tells make frequent reference to bridegrooms and bridesmaids, and he calls himself the bridegroom (see, for instance, Mt. 25:1-13; Lk.5:34). We should not forget that Jesus' very first miracle in John's Gospel is at a wedding in Cana where he greatly blesses the celebration (Jn. 2:1-11). However, Jesus also suggests that whoever does not leave behind father and mother for his sake is not worthy of the kingdom of heaven (Mt. 10:32-38). When Jesus' own mother and brothers appear outside the door where he is teaching, Jesus proclaims that his mother and brothers are those who do his will, not those who have blood relationships with him (Mt. 12:46-50). Jesus does not offer a case either for marriage or celibacy. If there is a theme that goes through the Gospel accounts, it is that Jesus has a view toward a much larger goal: faithful discipleship to Christ himself. Such faithful discipleship takes place in the context of faithful marriages or faithful service as celibates in the kingdom of God.

If the Gospels are confusing on whether one should be married or celibate, the rest of the New Testament is no less so. Paul's famous passage in 1 Corinthians 7 acclaims celibacy as the way to properly focus attention on the work we do for Jesus. Marriage appears as a stopgap in this letter; it is for those who would otherwise burn with lust. In other letters, however, marriages and households become exceedingly important. Paul even suggests that marriage between a man and a woman is like the marriage between Christ and the church (Eph. 5:32), which is why fidelity and vows are so important to Christians. The New Testament ends with John's Revelation, in which the Bridegroom, the Lamb, figures heavily, and in which the marriage of the church and the Lamb is proclaimed (Rev. 19:7-9). Both marriage and celibacy are exalted; both marriage and celibacy are seen as means toward the goal Jesus Christ has in mind: the kingdom of God. Thus, neither state of life should be seen as having a different ultimate purpose than the other.

What should be clear in this all too brief survey of Scriptural witness about marriage and celibacy is that there is no law to follow here. Celibacy may indeed be better than marriage, via Paul, but marriage cannot be tossed aside lightly as having no merit. Indeed, both can be positive ways to respond to God. Because there is no law in either case (for more on this, see Paul's exhortation in 1 Cor. 7), what is most definitely needed is the help of the community for discerning and faithfully living these states of life.

III. Communities Supporting Celibacy and Marriage

This eighth mark of a new monasticism is eschatological, which means that marriage and celibacy are always supposed to make us aware of who we are, whose we are, and where we are going as God's people. The first two ways I suggest for living out the eighth mark are based directly on what the text says. The mark carefully states that we are to support *celibate* people and *monogamous married* couples and their children. In other words, not every kind of relationship is okay in intentional communities.

Accountability

My first vital but difficult suggestion for communities is to hold people accountable to practicing relationships that are life-giving and Christ-bearing. This is excruciatingly difficult, because peoples' relationships bear some of the strongest emotional, cultural and social ties. (A most visible example of this is an abusive relationship where neither party finds the will to leave.) Communities that dare to be involved in relationship accountability and support of the kind the Scriptures and this mark suggests should be aware of and prepared for the ensuing mess. I have known of more than one Christian community that has had to exhort someone who was committing adultery, for instance.

Nonetheless, if we believe that even the way we live in relationship with each other (married or celibate) is important to following Christ and seeking his kingdom, we should be involved in fostering relationships. This will mean fostering all the kinds of relationships that exist in community, between married couples, friends, enemies, and members of the whole group. Each community will need to find ways to do this that are particular to themselves. One community in Kentucky requests that people who are married not find themselves alone with members of the opposite sex who are not their spouses. Another community in North Carolina allotted time in its weekly meetings for people who had had a falling out to speak with each other and reach some understanding.

Communities may find that they need extra help in carrying out this step. When Benedict wrote his rule for monasteries, he included the office of an abbot, someone whose word was final, not because he or she was necessarily better than the rest but because that person was "elected for merit of life and learnedness in wisdom" and had teachings "sprinkled with the ferment of divine justice." This was a person who was elected by the community and seen as someone who could deal fairly and well with the messiness of relationships in communities. New monastic communities may want to consider adding such an office to their own rules. Alternatively, Chris Rice writes in his book *Grace Matters* that his community in Mississippi needed to call on the help of people external to the community in order to find help.

Discernment

A second suggestion, closely related to the first, is that communities need to help people think through their relationships by setting up discernment practices for both states of life (e.g. dating, novitiate, engagement, etc.). This, too, is difficult. As a friend of mine once quipped, "It's easier for us to tell each other what kind of car to buy than who to marry." Many churches already do these kinds of discernment practices in premarital counseling seminars; almost all monastic communities have some sort of discernment process with a novice master concerning celibacy. New monastic communities may want to base their own practices of discernment on these two groups. A small intentional Christian community of college students in Colorado Springs helped people discern on a much smaller scale by asking one person in the community to have conversations with all those who were considering marriage or monastic vows as they prepared for graduation. These conversations were tailored to the individual's specific situation; sometimes the conversations were about concerns with the potential future spouse (e.g. not egalitarian enough; too irresponsible) and some conversations involved thinking through what it would mean to take vows or to give up the idea of marriage altogether.

Parenting

My third suggestion involves the last part of the eighth mark: communities should be about supporting monogamous married couples and their *children*. I stated in the first two sections that the primary importance of marriage and celibacy is that these are states of life that lead us toward God's kingdom. Therefore, both states of life involve thinking theologically. This is no different when it comes to children. The Triune God loves and blesses children and sees them as quite capable of carrying out the work of the kingdom. Jeremiah protested that he was too young to be a prophet, but God called him anyway (Jer. 1:6). Jesus welcomed children and proclaimed that they would inherit the kingdom of God (Mt. 21:16; Mk. 13-14). Moreover, intentional Christian communities are related to the churches of which they are part. Whether those churches baptize children or dedicate them, a high value is placed on their care and the congregation is admonished to raise them as Christians. Intentional Christian communities assume that responsibility as well. Celibates and married people both need to be responsible for raising children.

A small Catholic Worker house in Indiana has discovered this in some poignant ways. At first, it housed mostly men; then it branched out to house women and their children because they recognized the poverty that confounds single women with children. The community discovered that the children they lived with lagged behind their peers when they began school in the first grade because their parents were absent or unable to help. So some of the celibate people in the community began an informal, short, daily "preschool" for the younger children they lived with, along with the children of married members. This "preschool" now largely involves helping children interact with each other in order to learn basic speaking skills, social skills, and self-care skills such as tying shoes. The celibate people found that regardless of whether they themselves had biologically borne children, they had a responsibility to raise them.

Openness

Whether or not we live in communities where celibates and married people live together, we need to be intentional about forming relationships and seeking out the gifts and graces of the other state of life. Communities of single, celibate people should not be closed off from communities of married people, and communities that house people from both states of life ought to consider ways to be intentional about including gifts and graces from both states. I will close by showing how my own community, a group of single people practicing celibacy (though not vowed celibacy), tries to do this. Several friends and acquaintances of the community are married couples with children. We encourage these families to come to our house and we make dinner, offering toys to the children as well as good conversation to the adults. This is a simple way to give home-cooked meals and support to oft-harried families. Often the conversation turns to a discussion of how our community life is going (be it the marriage/family community or the intentional community in which

I live). Some of the disagreements and problems are similar, and we learn from each other. Sometimes the problems are different; we learn from that, too. Through all these get-togethers, we try to remember that each state of life exhibits the life of Christ for the world and we try to help each other on that path.

Mark 9: Geographical Proximity to Community Members Who Share a Common Rule of Life

Jon Stock

I. Where I Live

Since 1987, I have lived in an intentional community. Currently, my household is made up of 13 people, one dog, two cats, and a pig (the pig and the cats stay outside). This is a little more crowded than usual for us, but Christian friendship, a sense of humor, and the merciful rhythms of God's community make it a joyful household in which to live. Our congregation is made up of seven houses within five minutes walking distance from each other. This close proximity was very intentional, and it continues to be an expectation placed on all members of our community.

We have never claimed a biblical injunction for proximity. Our decision to live with and near one another is a very practical idea based upon modern American urban culture. For us, making the very practical step of moving close to one another has everything to do with issues of identity and mission. Many Americans derive identity from family, neighborhood, employment, or hobbies. We are trying to live in such a way that our identity as members of Christ's church is primary. Moving in order to be close to one another was a clear way of marking our new identity in Christ with his church. Living close together also enables us to work together to create a space within which we can nurture an atmosphere that tastes and smells like the Kingdom of God. For us, creation of this particular type of space fulfills our vision for mission. In our view proclamation of the gospel rings shallow if we have no place to bring those who yearn to be immersed in the ways of the Kingdom of God.

To be sure, living in close proximity guarantees nothing. It is not some magic practice that will make all well. My experience is simply that proximity can and will enable other formative practices of discipleship – but individuals must still choose to give themselves to such practices.

II. Rooting the Mark in Scripture and Tradition

The commitment to geographical proximity is primarily a consequence of other practices, beliefs, ends, or marks. In other words, this mark is only intelligible as it functions in relationship to the other marks. For some this mark appears to be just another senseless rule. However, if you are committed to spiritual disciplines like common prayer, common meals, mutual confession of sins, spiritual guidance, and celebration, then geographical proximity is a great catalyst. As such, it is a means to the end of faithfully being the church. It is not the end itself, though it is especially, perhaps uniquely, suited to that end. Christian communes of the 1960s and 1970s occasionally lost sight of this distinction, overestimating the value of proximity for its own sake. Moving close to one another often ends up being the easy step. But it loses its significance if it is not connected to a committed openness to the other. In a sense proximity can form us to be open toward the other, which is what hospitality is all about. But it is no guarantee.

I think it is fair to say that our Scriptures do not include any commandment to live within close proximity. My point is that proximity is a consequence of the purpose and mission of the church, especially in our day of rampant self-centeredness. Nevertheless, Scripture does provide some key ecclesial concepts that provide some rationale for geographical proximity.

The primary biblical-theological concept underlying the practice of geographical proximity in the New Testament is that of *koinonia*. This Greek word is usually translated as "fellowship." Popular images of "fellowship" in many churches are limited to opportunities for light social interaction like the coffee hour, the potluck, or the Friday night singles group gathering. New Testament writers such as Luke or Paul had something much deeper in mind when they used the word *koinonia*.

A standard Greek dictionary will offer such definitions of *koinonia* as "communion," "association," "partnership," or "society." The word had a rich and varied meaning. It could be used to speak of a business partnership, a voluntary association, marriage, or the foundation of the cosmos. We must be careful not to hang our understanding of *koinonia* on any one word or concept, nor should we refuse to see that even its shallower meanings implied a partnership of substance.

To get a feel for the ways in which the New Testament uses the word *koinonia*, consider the following passages:

Acts 2:42   "They devoted themselves to the apostles' teaching and to the *koinonia*, to the breaking of bread and the prayers."

I Cor.1:9   "God is faithful; by him you were called into the *koinonia* of his son, Jesus Christ our Lord."

I Cor. 10:16   "The cup of blessing that we bless, is it not a *koinonia* in the blood of Christ? The bread that we break, is it not a *koinonia* in the body of Christ?"

II Cor. 6:14   "Do not be mismatched with unbelievers. For what partnership is there between righteousness and lawlessness? Or what *koinonia* is there between light and darkness?"

Gal. 2:9	"and when James and Cephas and John, who were acknowledged pillars, recognized the grace that had been given to me, they gave to Barnabas and me the right hand of *koinonia*, agreeing that we should go to the Gentiles and they go to the circumcised."
Phil. 3:10	"I want to know Christ and the power of his resurrection and the *koinonia* of the sufferings by becoming like him in his death."
Heb. 13:16	"Do not neglect the doing of good and *koinonia* for such sacrifices are pleasing to God."
I John 1:3	"we declare to you what we have seen and heard so that you also may have *koinonian* with us; and truly our *koinonia* is with the Father and with his son Jesus Christ."

While it is certainly not true of every *koinos* or *koinonia* usage in the New Testament[1], we do need to see that *koinonia* speaks primarily to "mutual participation." In Christ, Christians not only belong to one another but actually become mutually identified, truly rejoicing with the happy and genuinely weeping with the sad. Christians give to one another because they belong to one another. Christians mutually participate in Christ. Christians "mutually indwell" one another. Although this is a spiritual reality, it necessarily takes concrete, bodily expression. It involves whole persons, including bodies, minds, and emotions. It seems

---

[1] It is certainly the case that *koinonia* in NT is both local and universal. For example, sending gifts to Paul in prison is seen as *koinonia* in his sufferings. The collection for famine relief in Jerusalem is also seen as *koinonia*. In other words, exchanging gifts (mostly financial) seemed to be a way of extending local *koinonia* across large spatial distances or large theological distances in the sense that Jewish Christians in Jerusalem accepting financial relief from Pauline Gentile churches seemed also to imply accepting them as fellow Christians.

clear to me that the New Testament expects our *koinonia* to be quite physical, implying a sharing of time, money, possessions and our very selves. We serve together; we share money; we borrow and lend automobiles; we celebrate with those who are happy; we mourn with those who are sad.

The church would look quite different today if we began to infuse the meaning of *koinonia* into our language of "fellowship." We would begin to see that our ecclesial life is one of much greater shared communion. We would begin to see that the nature of our relationships ought to be deeper than we have supposed. We would begin to see that our commitment to one another should be taken more seriously. If we understood *koinonia* better, the mark of geographical proximity would make more sense to us.

Allelon is a Greek reciprocal pronoun that means "one another." It is a frequently overlooked concept and we often miss its significance for the New Testament church and for us. Although far from exhaustive, consider the following list of passages from the New Testament epistles:

Rom. 12:16	"live in harmony with one another"
Rom. 15:14	"admonish one another"
I Cor. 12:25	"have the same care for one another"
Gal. 5:13	"be servants of one another"
Gal. 6:2	"bear one another's burdens"
I Thess. 5:11	"comfort one another...build one another up"
I Thess. 5:13	"be at peace with one another...do good to one another"
Eph. 4:2	"bear with one another lovingly"
Eph. 4:32	"be kind and compassionate to one another"
Eph. 5:21	"be subject to one another"
Col. 3:13	"forgive one another"
James 5:16	"confess your sins to one another"
I Pet. 4:9	"be hospitable to one another"[2]

---

[2] This draws heavily on the fine work of Gerhard Lohfink in *Jesus and Community* pp. 99ff. I heavily recommend this work for anyone who wants to read further on what Lohfink calls "the Praxis of Togetherness."

The "one-another" passages are a clear call to a life of togetherness and mutual participation. How can the church live into these admonitions of Paul and Peter and James unless it actually sees each other more than just weekly? How can we practice this life of togetherness when our commitment of proximity to work or to school is more important than proximity to fellow members of our Christian congregation? The scriptures clearly call the people of God to participate in the abundant life of togetherness. Geographical proximity is the great enabler of the call to togetherness.

"If we say that we have *koinonian* with him while we are walking in darkness, we lie and do not do what is true; but if we walk in the light as he himself is in the light, we have *koinonian* with *allelon*, and the blood of Jesus his Son cleanses us from all sin" (I John 1.6-7).

III. Stories from Communities of New Monasticism

Below are short pictures of communities or congregations for which geographical proximity is important to their churchly mission. I've attempted to represent each in their own words. For each the mark of geographical proximity plays an important role in their corporate life, though they each have a unique congregational vision or location.

Church of the Sojourners: San Francisco, California
Church of the Sojourners is located in the midst of San Francisco's Mission District, a neighborhood known for its number of poor Central American immigrants. The mission of the Church of the Sojourners is simply to be the Body of Christ together. For the past twenty years they have lived in shared housing within blocks of one another, sharing in ministry to their neighborhood and to one another. Each week they eat evening meals together, engage in worship and Bible study, meet in accountability and prayer groups, and share a rich life of partnership.

The Church of the Sojourners has attempted to build up traditions and celebrations that give them more of a feeling of being a "people" or a "family." They are working at transforming their primary identity from that of "American" or "stock-broker" to that of "follower of Christ." Their commitment to live near one another enables them to construct a common identity and mission centered around the gospel. They see themselves as being called out of the North American culture in order to witness to the possibility of a different way of life, an existence in the world determined more by the light of the gospel than the darkness around them. They attempt to reject the cultural values of independence, rights-based thinking, and self-fulfillment in favor of a commitment to letting themselves be crucified with Christ. In addition to the practices mentioned above, they sustain their interdependence by taking retreats and vacations together, sharing economic resources, and living in close proximity to one another.

Their vision as a church is to keep on growing up into the fullness of the stature of our Lord Jesus Christ. They don't have a lot of specifics attached to this besides loving one another, repenting of their sin, and showing forth God's love to the world around them.

Christ Community Church: Des Moines, Iowa

When Christ Community Church in Des Moines, Iowa gathers on Sundays for worship, they look like many suburban congregations around America. They have recently become affiliated with the Mennonite Church, but were originally part of a free-church, Protestant "mega-church." Underneath the initial Sunday morning impression, one finds something much deeper going on in this congregation. These folk in Iowa have begun to creatively address the call to discipleship in the context of suburban middle-America. Approximately 85% of the congregation is involved in house churches. Christ Community Church makes it clear to those interested in membership that "house church" is part of the way that they do church.

As much as is possible, the people who make up a house

church live in geographic proximity to each other. They meet weekly following Sunday morning worship in homes around the city/suburbs. They continue to gather throughout the week for common life and ministry. The house churches attempt to develop a ministry in the context of the immediate neighborhood in which they live.

Some of them have been working at moving even closer to each other by selling existing homes and purchasing new ones closer to one another. Others are making plans for living together in the same house/house church.

This is not merely a voluntary small group ministry. This is an earnest attempt to be the church by being closer to one another. Each house church undertakes a covenanted way of life. Below is the covenant that they share together:

Why Should We Have A House Church Covenant?
Our God is a covenant-making, covenant-keeping God. In Jesus Christ, God established his New Covenant with all who are baptized into Jesus' name. In our membership with a body of Christian believers, God saves us from the kingdom of evil and places us under his own loving reign. This is not to say the church saves. Jesus saves, but our salvation has a churchly shape. In other words, our relatedness to other Christians is not something extra to Christianity – it is the very shape of the New Covenant into which we were baptized. In Christ, God reconciles us to himself *and to each other*.

We who were reconciled through baptism have not only been saved *from* evil; we have been saved *into* the mission of Christ. All Christians share in the mission of reconciling the world to God in Christ. Since this mission is too difficult for any of us alone, God has chosen other people to work with us. These are the people whose faces we see when we look around Christ Community Church. Perhaps they are not the faces we would have chosen for ourselves! Nevertheless, the Holy Spirit has brought us together. In order to display God's reconciling work, local groups of Christians should commit themselves to loving each other with the very love of God's New Covenant in Christ. Without such a bond between us, we fail to show the world how God is reuniting the fragmented human race.

House Church is one of the primary settings where we live out our commitment as members of Christ Community Church. House Church is not merely a "program" of Christ Community Church. Indeed, we believe we cannot fully experience the common life of Christ Community Church without being united to a smaller, more intimate group. Therefore, if we have committed ourselves to membership in Christ Community Church, then we should also commit ourselves to a House Church.

This covenant should not be viewed as confinement, although it does require from us a deep commitment to each other. By living in faithful, steadfast love with each other, we *strengthen* each other for the mission of Christ and *liberate* each other to serve God without fear.

House Church Covenant

In light of these truths, we pledge to *give priority* in our lives to the *shared mission* of reconciling the world to God in Christ. This mission will involve our time, resources, affections and relationships – indeed, all that we are and have.

Therefore, by God's grace we will:

- Faithfully *meet* together in our homes each week to cultivate our common life in Christ;
- Gladly *make time* for each other and for our shared mission to the world;
- Cheerfully *share* our possessions with each other and with the poor;
- Joyfully *work* together to advance God's reign of justice, love and peace in the world;

- Truthfully *speak* words of encouragement and admonition to each other;
- Humbly *submit* to each other in love and mutual service, recognizing each other's gifts and respecting the leadership that God has ordained;
- Patiently *listen* to each other, *confess* our sins to each other, and *bear* each other's burdens;
- Mercifully *forgive* each other as God in Christ forgave us.

These actions describe how Christ has loved us. By the empowerment of his Holy Spirit, we will strive to love each other in the same way, so the world may know and care that Jesus is Lord. We commit ourselves to this covenant for the next year, or until we mutually discern that a change in our relationship is warranted by God's design.

Temescal Commons: Oakland, California

Temescal Commons is a small Christian community in Oakland, California. They seek to create more simplified, integrated lifestyles to care for their neighborhood and their neighbors, and to appreciate and steward God's creation by using well the resources they have. To further these goals, the folks at Temescal Commons have designed their physical site with community and sustainability in mind, using environmentally-friendly building materials and conservation technology and creating shared yards, gardens, cooking, dining, and laundry areas.

The Temescal Commons project originated in 1996, when a group of Rockridge United Methodist Church members began talking about living together in north Oakland. In the fall of 1997, they bought the 11,300 square foot lot, and soon thereafter, completed the project's design in collaboration with architects from The CoHousing Company. The site consists of a small cluster of nine housing units that includes an 1880s two-story house, which has been rehabilitated into two flats, as well as new construction consisting of a single-family unit, a duplex, a common house with an upstairs flat, and an existing triplex on adjacent property.

The detail design and construction process took approximately two years from the point of approval by their local Planning Commission to move-in. Throughout the planning, design, and construction process, the group came together for periodic workdays to demolish old structures, clear the lot, and renovate the old house. Each home is now owned as a condominium and a Homeowners Association assesses monthly dues to cover common area maintenance, utilities, and long-term replacement reserves.

The community includes singles and families, owners and renters. Their common life is anchored by two shared meals each week, monthly workdays, and bi-monthly all-community meetings. Owners also meet every other month and serve as the Association Board. They've found that their proximity to each other creates opportunities to gather for prayer and conversation and help each other in daily life. In these ways, they find God to be at work among them, nurturing and deepening their faith.

The Bruderhof

The Bruderhof began in Germany in the aftermath of World War I, when Dr. Eberhard Arnold, a well-known public speaker, left the comforts of Berlin and moved to the tiny village of Sannerz with his wife and children. There they sought to flesh out their vision of a society in which love and justice replace violence, isolation, and greed.

In the early 1930s, the community came into direct conflict with Germany's Nazi government. As a Gestapo official noted, the Bruderhof "represents a world-view totally opposed to National Socialism."

Harboring Jews—and refusing to serve in the German army, accept a Nazi schoolteacher, or use the "Heil Hitler" salute—the community soon became the target of harassment and open persecution. In 1937, secret police surrounded the community, imprisoned several members, and gave the rest forty-eight hours to leave the country.

Neighboring Liechtenstein offered temporary refuge but could not permanently protect the Bruderhof from the threat of Nazism. Fortunately, an influx of British guests opened doors in England, and the community was able to purchase a derelict farm in the Cotswolds and relocate there.

Even before the outbreak of the Second World War, the community's German members (and the pacifist stance of its English ones) attracted deep suspicion locally. Economic boycotts were organized, and soon it become impossible to survive. When confronted with the option of either interning all German members, or leaving England as a group, the Bruderhof chose the latter and began to look for refuge abroad.

The Bruderhof sought entry in many countries including the United States and Canada, but because its members came from both Axis and Allied countries, asylum was repeatedly denied. Finally, with the help of American Mennonites, the community found refuge in Paraguay. Getting several hundred people across the submarine-infested Atlantic was a chapter in itself, but amazingly, everyone reached South America safely.

In 1954, in response to growing interest in community living in America, Woodcrest Bruderhof was founded in Rifton, New York. New communities were also founded in Pennsylvania (1957) and Connecticut (1958). At the same time, although the Paraguayan communities were now thriving, a growing frustration with their isolation and inaccessibility resulted in their closing. By 1962, all members had relocated to the northeastern United States or to England.

The largest Bruderhof has over four hundred members; the smallest has about twenty. But each one follows the same daily rhythm, and has the same basic departments, including a nursery, kindergarten, school, a communal kitchen, laundry, various workshops, and offices.

Bruderhof life is built around the family. Children are an important part of each community and participate in most communal gatherings.

All life is regarded as precious. Disabled and elderly members are loved and cared for within the community and participate in daily life and work for as long as they are able.

Communal work is an important part of daily life and takes place primarily at the Bruderhof, whether in the central kitchen, daycare, or laundry, or in one of the community's businesses.

No Bruderhof member receives a salary or has a bank account. Income from all businesses is pooled and used for the care of all members, and for various communal outreach efforts.

Campfires, hikes, softball games, and other recreational activities provide opportunities for communal interaction, as do outdoor work projects such as hauling firewood. Technology is used when it aids efficiency and communication—but not if it robs members of meaningful work. Manual skills are valued and encouraged, whether for hobbies such as pottery or gardening, or in fields such as welding, carpentry, and landscaping.

In a world of loneliness and discord, countless people long for community, and the Bruderhof's life together is an expression of that longing. Their goal is to overcome the isolation and fragmentation that mark our time by fighting their root cause—selfishness—in themselves.

Working and eating communally, sharing houses and cars, raising their children together, and helping each other in the care of disabled and aged loved ones, the Bruderhof seek to live an organic life that addresses the needs of every individual yet still serves a greater common good.

Proximity guarantees nothing, but it does enable practices that are easily lost in the suburban dream. I hope that I have at least stimulated further exploration of the ways in which living closer to one another can be a faithful response to God's call to his people.

Mark 10: Care for the Plot of God's Earth Given to Us Along with Support of Our Local Economies

Norman Wirzba

I. The Conspiracy to Murder Creation

It came as a real shock to me the first time I read Wendell Berry's claim that "The certified Christian seems just as likely as anyone else to join the military-industrial conspiracy to murder Creation."[1] Growing up in the farming communities of southern Alberta, in full view of the Canadian Rockies, my sense of creation was majestic, unspoiled wilderness. The beauty of these mountains, forests, lakes, clouds, and the diverse array of wildlife they contained, fairly sang out the chorus of the Psalmist: "The heavens are telling the glory of God; and the firmament proclaims his handiwork" (19:1). It made perfect sense to me to think that the splendor of nature, extending from the starry sky to the creeping things on the ground, resounded in praise to the Creator who made them and daily sustains them (see Psalms 148 and 104:27-30). It didn't seem possible that creation was in much danger. It looked, sounded, smelled, felt, and tasted too good to be embroiled in murderous death.

---

[1] Wendell Berry. "Christianity and the Survival of Creation," in *The Art of the Commonplace: The Agrarian Essays of Wendell Berry*, ed. Norman Wirzba (Washington: Counterpoint, 2002), p.306.

137

Moreover, my family, as well as most of the Christians I knew, was involved in farming, an occupation that I thought flowed seamlessly from God's injunction at the dawn of time to "till and keep" the Garden of Eden (Genesis 2:15). We were not destroyers of land and animal life. We cared for the soil, tended our crops, and looked after our animals with as much attention as the next farmer. It would not be going too far to say that a good measure, though certainly not all, of the work I experienced bore witness to a fundamental affection for creation. Looking back, I would have been hard-pressed to identify these farming communities as co-conspirators in the ways of death.

Despite my idyllic reminiscences, however, I must admit that Berry is correct. The evidence of murder is simply too overwhelming. The wilderness habitats that I so much love are almost everywhere in serious decline due to careless human encroachment, resource extraction, invasive pests, and toxins/pollutants of bewildering variety. Wildlife species are disappearing at an alarming and unprecedented rate as their habitats shrink or vanish altogether. The sight of an old growth forest, the sound of a loon, and the aroma of a wild rose are today just as likely to be interrupted by the scars of a clear-cut logging operation, the whine of an all-terrain vehicle or Jet-Ski, and the stench of a copper smelting plant. Even the farm fields I have occasion to walk over now betray the signs of fatigue, erosion, salination, soil compaction, and microbial death. The animals, if I see them at all, live mostly in confinement operations that severely impair their freedom to be. The farmers themselves are mostly old, living in communities that more and more resemble ghost towns or rural ghettos.

My growth into adulthood, my putting away the naïve visions of youthful innocence, has forced me to look more honestly at the world and there confront the awful destructiveness of our economic ways. We no longer have the luxury of bracketing our world into neat compartments, of focusing on the beautiful, calendar-like settings of Lake Louise, and then forgetting (or hiding from) the ugly, ravaged landscapes of places like Camden, New

Jersey. What we need is to see and engage creation with clarity and honesty, and then determine if our own creative, economic life honors, respects, and celebrates the Creator's own work. How much does our current "high quality" of life, the life enjoyed by many contemporary Christians, depend upon the exploitation and disregard of whole swaths of creation? How, given the widespread belief in God as the Creator of the world, have we gotten to the point where we (sometimes blindly, sometimes knowingly) destroy and disfigure so much of the Creator's handiwork? What we obviously lack is a clear sense of the natural and human worlds *as creation*.

II. Creation Care in Scripture and Tradition

Scripture gives a surprisingly rich and nuanced account of the world as creation.[2] Sadly, however, much of this account has gone unnoticed by us because we think the meaning of this doctrine is exhausted in a description of the origins of the universe. The full significance of the teaching of creation emerges as we see it establishing a moral and spiritual topography in which all of life, human and non-human, is situated within the intentions of God's own life. Here we discover not only where we came from, but also where we—people, coyotes, ducks, lilacs, earthworms, glaciers—are going and how (morally speaking) we are to get there. The doctrine of creation aims to show us how our life grows out of God's love and is directed toward God's joy and delight. The whole world, as Hildegard of Bingen said, was fashioned to be adored and to be showered with God's gifts of love. It testifies to an all-embracing divine kiss. And so creation is not simply something that God did long ago. It is, rather, the arena in which God's presence and power, as well as God's care, are continually being worked out. Made in the image of God, we bear a special responsibility to make sure that our own work resonates and harmonizes

---

[2] For a fuller treatment of the biblical material discussed here see chapter 1 of my book *The Paradise of God: Renewing Religion in an Ecological Age* (New York: Oxford University Press, 2003).

with this care. If we fail, as when we mercilessly degrade and destroy creation's ability to flourish as God wants, or when we choose to be ignorant of the deadly effects of our economic practices, then we rightly deserve to be called co-conspirators and murderers.

Our propensity for murder, of course, is written into the earliest creation story. Adam, having been fashioned out of the same ground (*adamah*) as all the other creatures, is commanded to keep and serve the needs of the "garden of delights." Together with his family, he is instructed to make sure that his work preserves the gifts of life generously given by God. This is what it means to be a creature, namely to conserve and maintain the processes of life that bring delight and joy to the Creator. Adam and Eve, however, are not content with their roles of creatureliness. They want to be little gods themselves and take life into their own hands. The tragic consequences of their rebellion become full-blown in the lives of their sons as Cain murders Abel. The garden of delight cannot abide our violent natures, and so humans are expelled.

Our temptation has been to end the creation story here with the expulsion from the garden. But the narrative thread of this story goes much further, extending all the way to the life of Noah. It is important that we not stop the creation story with the generation of Cain and Abel because if we do we miss out on what is most important about God's promise and intent for creation. Whereas Adam and Eve introduced failure and sin into the life of creation, Noah and his family will stand out as beacons of faithfulness, as models of what it means for people to fully embrace their roles as creatures made in the image of God. Noah, it turns out, demonstrates in his own living why we are here, shows where God wants us to go, and models what we need to do to get there.

The violence and degradation that marked the generations following Adam and Eve form the immediate context for Noah's own life. Noah is chosen by God to show us a different way, a way that returns us to our original command to serve/preserve/conserve the creation. Adopting this role would not be easy, however, especially given our propensity to want to be gods our-selves. And so Noah's education in the responsibilities and joys of authentic creatureliness would take place within the awful cir-cumstance of the destruction of the world itself. Humanity, having already compromised the integrity of creation through acts of hubris and violence, will now be tested to see whether or not it can be faithful to creation before God.

According to Rabbinic tradition we miss out on the real sig-nificance of the flood story if we see the ark as a rescue or escape vehicle. The true meaning of the ark experience is not that it gets Noah and two of all the animals through a time of drowning death. Rather, the ark represents the training ground in which Noah will learn what it means to be responsible for creation and faithful to God. What we need to think about is the humble atten-tion and care required of Noah and his family members simply so that the animals would not starve on the ark. In the ark the ani-mals were entirely dependent on Noah for their food and well-being. Had Noah not been responsible, i.e., had he not sub-mitted himself to a life of service to creation and faithfulness to God, they would have died the deaths of starvation and disease rather than drowning.

We do better, then, to think of the ark as a school for compas-sion and care, the testing/training ground in which the lessons of humanly authentic creatureliness could be learned and devel-oped. And lest we think that this work is onerous or beneath ourselves, we have the testimony of Rabbinic tradition which says that Noah's adoption of his God-given responsibilities brought so much joy and delight to Noah that he did not sleep during the several months of the ark experience. He didn't want to sleep because he might then miss out on opportunities to maintain and enhance the lives of his fellow creatures, and thus experience the pleasures that come from such care.

When Noah and the creatures finally do emerge from the ark it is an emergence marked by faithfulness to God. Where Adam and Eve had failed, Noah succeeded because he understood that human life is but a part of God's creation, and that God desires the health and wholeness of all creation. Creation does not simply exist to serve our excessive wants. Rather, we exist to maintain the gifts of God. We do this best when, like Noah, we make ourselves into the servants of others, looking after their needs. Noah is the authentic person because he restores the connection between *adam* and *adamah*, the connection between humanity and life-giving soil (indeed, Noah, after being divinely blessed and commanded much like Adam before him, is proclaimed the "first tiller of the soil," (9:20) despite generations of farmers who preceded him, because he engaged creation with care and compassion). Until we take up our divinely appointed task of caring for creation, the delight that marked God's original creative work will continue to be distorted and denied.

Another scriptural tradition in which the moral and spiritual topography of creation becomes clear is to be found in the Sabbath legislation. Many of us associate Sabbath observance with resting or "taking a break" from the frantic schedules we normally keep for ourselves. After all, didn't God even find the need to rest from the labors of creating the world? If we look at the scriptural text a little more carefully we discover that there is more to the Sabbath than simple inaction or ceasing from work. Why is it that we are told that God finished creating on the sixth day only to read that on the seventh day God finished *again* the creation of the world (Genesis 2:1-2)? Was there something left uncreated on the seventh day? According to Rabbinic tradition what was left uncreated was *menuha*, the tranquility, peace, and serenity that marked creation in its origin. Without *menuha* creation would not be complete. It would be a mass of habitats and organisms without a divine, overarching purpose. The creation of *menuha* means that all of life finds its meaning and goal in the delight of God.

If we are to understand properly the full meaning of creation, and thus also our proper place within it, we must know what its purpose or goal is. Throughout much of our religious history we have assumed that because humanity is created last, and because we are created in the image of God, that we are the most important members of creation. What is lower serves what is higher. And so we have designed cultures that thrive at the expense of the rest of creation: energy production at the expense of strip mining, suburban sprawl at the cost of lost farmland, cheap food at the expense of soil fertility, and economic development for the price of species extinction. We justify these practices by saying that God made the creation for our enjoyment.

Israelite experience shows us that this understanding of the Sabbath is seriously flawed. What we are to learn from Sabbath observance is precisely the opposite, namely that creation does not exist solely for our own benefit. When we ruthlessly dominate it we bring ruin to ourselves and the creation as a whole. This message became very clear in the context of the Israelite wandering in the wilderness, the place in which the Sabbath code first developed. What the Israelites most needed to learn is that they are not in control of their histories, and that their lives are not to do with as they pleased. God is in control, and it is upon God that we must perpetually and joyfully rely for our well-being. Their instruction took a most practical form: manna as food rained down from heaven. Each day the Israelites were to collect enough manna for the day. Those who tried to collect more (perhaps out of greed, unfaithfulness, or the desire to capitalize on another's vulnerability) would find that the manna had spoiled. But on the sixth day they were to collect a double portion so that they could devote time on the seventh day to worship God, give thanks for the many gifts of creation, and be refreshed by the acknowledgment of countless blessings (Exodus 16). Insofar as the Israelites succeeded in responsibly and faithfully enjoying the gifts of creation, they experienced a taste of what creation is finally about, the *menuha* of God.

To careful observers it is plain to see that creation today does not exhibit the peace, delight, and tranquility that marked the very first sunrise. In large part the languishing of our world is attributable to our abuse of it. We have subverted the purposes of living things to meet our own wants rather than to bring delight to God. The question we need to ask, therefore, is what structural changes in our economies are needed so that we together with God can once again experience *menuha*. The significance of this question should not be underestimated, particularly when we remember that according to a Rabbinic tradition, if we ever truly or authentically celebrate the Sabbath even once, the Messiah will come.

Christians, who believe that Jesus is the Messiah, have much to add to this understanding of the Sabbath because we affirm that Jesus is the lord of the Sabbath. What this means is that Sabbath life finds its most concrete and practical manifestation in Jesus' ministries of feeding the hungry, healing the sick, restoring the broken and deranged, even raising the dead. Insofar as we continue in these ministries—is this not precisely what the vocation of the church is?—we continue to be a Sabbath presence in the world, testifying to the ways of *menuha* rather than the ways of destruction and death.

With these two brief scriptural accounts of Noah and the Sabbath we can now see that the teaching of creation is much richer than accounts about the origins of the world would suggest. The doctrine of creation introduces us to the moral and spiritual *character* of the world and invites us to become faithful participants in the aims and purposes of the Creator. Above all what these accounts communicate is that we are most ourselves when we embrace our creatureliness and cease trying to be gods, when we practice care and service to creation and faithfulness before God. All other paths lead to sin and our continuing expulsion from the garden.

In our culture it will not be easy for us to act out our creatureliness. In part this is because the idea that creation exists primarily for our benefit has been so thoroughly ingrained in our habits and thinking. We have gotten used to the idea that the natural world has no value until we assign it one. If we are to make any progress in the ways of restoring creation we do best if we start by developing concrete practices that affirm and make manifest our responsibility before God to serve and maintain the wholeness of creation. Four practices in particular can serve as a useful beginning point.

III. *Four Practices for the New Monasticism*

Grow a garden

One of the main reasons for our disregard of creation is that we no longer feel ourselves intimately bound up with biological processes of life and death. As we have become more urbanized we have also come to believe that we exist apart from biological processes altogether. Food has become a mere commodity, fuel to get us through the day. The palpable identification between humanity and soil (*adam* from *adamah*) is lost on us. Growing vegetable gardens, besides providing us with nutritious and healthy food, will remind us again that we live from the soil, and that our own health depends on its health. Tending gardens will teach us that life does not proceed according to our own often frantic and life-denying schedules, but according to the rhythms of growth, rest, disease, death, and rebirth. Gardening will introduce us to the miracle of God's continuing presence in the ways of life. So often we think that miracles occur in the supernatural realm when in fact they occur around us all the time in places like soil that transform dead bodies into new organic life, or plants that transform sunshine into wheat.

Gardening, in other words, will teach us to trust less in our own might and to rely more on the grace of God. As every gardener knows, we are not the ones who control life. We can only prepare the way, through humble attention to the demands of weather, plant and insect life, topography, etc., and then let the grace and power of God take over. Too often our understanding of grace is abstract and motivated by selfish concern. Gardening will help restore in us a more honest experience of the blessings but also the terrors of grace. It will become an authentic basis for hope.

That we need this hope is painfully clear, particularly when we recall the ravaged landscapes of Camden, New Jersey or Chernobyl, Ukraine. These are the places in which unchecked human power and greed have done some of their worst damage by destroying soil and water with chemical toxins and nuclear poisons. How might God's grace become active and apparent in these places abused and abandoned by us? Fortunately, we have the example of dedicated urban gardeners like the new monastic community at Camden House who are gradually rehabilitating toxic sites so that they might once again become gardens reflecting God's grace. They are doing this by working with residents in the Camden community to grow tomatoes, lettuce, peas, and other vegetables. They are feeding bodies and souls at the same time as they model creaturely care and compassion to a world that has been consigned to the refuse heap of our culture.

Support local economies/shop responsibly

Christians have, often without knowing it, contributed to the destruction of creation because they have given their proxies to an economy that depends on the extraction and exhaustion of God's good gifts. We give these proxies every time we buy something at the store. When we remember, particularly in a global economy, that most of us never see the processes of production that make "goods" available to us, it is little wonder that we are in no position to make an honest judgment about whether or not consumer products were justly provided. What was the toll to natural and social environments making a product possible? Were workers humanely cared for and compensated? We need to understand and come to grips with the fact that we consume today with unprecedented ignorance about the causes and effects of our consumption.

Promoting and supporting local economies will go a long way to making sure that our production and consumption practices are carried out with greater justice and mercy. For instance, when I buy meat and eggs from Elmwood Stock Farm I know that the animals were treated in a careful and compassionate manner because I know Ann Bell as its farmer. I can visit and thus visibly see how she runs her farm. This I cannot do when I buy food products that travel an average of 1300 miles from "factory farms" that hide brutality, disease, and death. We have gotten to be very good at hiding from the effects of our consumer choices. We prefer not to know if our choosing is premised on the compromising or the unjust treatment of God's creation. It is time for us, like Noah, to take greater responsibility for the gifts that have been entrusted to us. We can do this best when we make things ourselves, buy locally produced goods, or, failing that, when we buy from manufacturers who we know to have the well-being of environments, workers, and consumers as a top priority.

Design generous households

The early church father John of Damascus once described God's creation as the work of "making room" for others to be and to share in the divine life. This is a beautiful way of highlighting the hospitable character of God's own creativity. As made in the image of God, it is our responsibility to exercise, on a smaller scale of course, similar acts of hospitality. We do this when we stop assuming that all of creation must give way to our own designs. Hosts are hospitable because they put the needs of their guests above their own. They share because they understand, even if not fully, how they are themselves the beneficiaries of a multitude of gifts and blessings.

To help us learn the ways of hospitality we can turn directly to creation itself. Soil, as every gardener knows, is a prime example of hospitality in that it makes room for another life to flourish and grow. Could we learn to design our economies and our households so that the well-being of others takes precedence over our own wants, as when we share household goods and services? As we all know, our homes are crammed with stuff we rarely use but nonetheless expensively purchase. We could readily relieve some of the stress that comes with ownership if we purchased products communally. Doing so would also take a great deal of the pressure off of environments that are feeling the pains of excessive extraction. As affluent Christians in North America, we have so much to give. In a world of diminishing resources it is a primary responsibility that we learn to share more and take less.

Practice celebration

If the goal of all created life is to participate in the *menuha* of God, then our most important work is practically to arrange our lives so that they lead to its full enjoyment and celebration. Indeed, what could be a clearer indication of our care for another than to work toward its own enjoyment? But if we are to become the celebrants of God's gifts and grace, we must first learn to slow down the frantic pace of our consumer lives. We must overwhelm the competitive, often cut-throat, character of our economic/professional striving with an ethos of compassion and attention so that the integrity and grace of creation will visibly emerge.

A welcome development in environmental circles testifying to this shift can be seen in the international appeal and growth of the Slow Food movement. Here producers and consumers, in deliberate contrast to the values of our fast food nation, are learning to appreciate and enjoy the gifts of carefully produced and lovingly prepared food. Factory farms, and all they represent, are repudiated so that soil, water, plant, and animal are given the respect they deserve. Eating becomes the occasion for celebration, and farming an opportunity to take the time to genuinely "serve and keep" creation.

Christians have every reason in the world to see their own lives and the lives of all those around them in terms of the gracious hospitality of God. It is as though we have all been invited to a lavish feast in which the Creator has proudly put on display the effects of an unimaginable love. Too often in our past we have entered the banquet as villains and murderers, as tyrants who want to claim as much for ourselves as possible. God calls us to enter it as fellow-creatures, as those who are willing to serve the well-being of each other, and then find in that service our unending joy and delight.

Mark 11: Peacemaking in the Midst of Violence and Conflict Resolution Along the Lines of Matthew 18

Fred Bahnson

"Pursue peace with everyone, and the holiness
without which no one will see the Lord."
Hebrews 12:14 NRSV[1]

I. My Own Journey to Peacemaking

I haven't always been a pacifist. I was once part of that vague majority of Christians in America who knew that Jesus said we're to love our enemies, but believed that doing so was "unrealistic." I thought Christians could, at times, use violence in the defense of justice. I lived in that tension between what Jesus commanded and what seemed to be a matter of "responsibility." Questions plagued me: *Isn't it wrong to "allow" innocent people to be killed if we can prevent it, even if that means killing the assailant? What about the Nazis? Jesus didn't really mean love* all *your enemies, did he?*

With a mix of evangelical, Christian Reformed, Lutheran, and Moravian in my family, I got to taste different slices of the Protestant pie. In none of these churches, however, did I hear about

---

[1]   All Scripture citations are from the NRSV

149

Christian nonviolence. In my hometown of Bozeman, Montana, good church people I knew supported the first Gulf War, even going to fight in it themselves. No one questioned why Christians were going off to kill for their country. That Christians followed the President's call simply came with the drinking water. I realize now that the predominant ethos in those churches regarding Christian use of force was a dualistic private/public morality—one I adopted as my own: we are to follow Jesus in our "private" lives, but in our "public" lives we have to act as the world does. You can turn the other cheek as an individual, but it's impossible to do that in "the public sphere." After all, sin is still present in the world, so violence is "necessary" to maintain order.

I eventually learned that Jesus explodes any distinction between personal and public morality, as if those two spheres could ever be separated. The shift in my thinking began in seminary where my studies convinced me that nonviolence is part of the life of discipleship that Jesus calls us to. But looking at the church's dismal history of acquiescence to violence, I couldn't see nonviolence enfleshed in real people. I had yet to see communities like those in the new monasticism that try to embody Christian pacifism. It was among *Las Abejas,* a small group of indigenous Christians in Chiapas, Mexico that I first saw Christian nonviolence practiced. But the story of *Las Abejas* and other communities who practice nonviolence will have to wait until Part III.

It is my prayer that Jesus will no longer weep for the American church as he wept over Jerusalem because she hasn't "recognized the things that make for peace" (Luke 19:42). American Christians shouldn't have to go to Mexico to find a faithful church. It is my prayer that the communities of the new monasticism can provide the kind of imaginative examples of Christian nonviolence that Christians in America sorely need.

II. Active Peacemaking and Cruciform Discipleship

Gospel Roots of Nonviolence
I grew up confused about how Christians deal with a violent

world because the church as a whole is confused. There is a startling disconnect between what the church preaches and how it lives. While the churches I grew up in were very good at *proclaiming* the gospel message of peace and reconciliation, our failure to *perform* that message negated anything we preached or printed.

The following example depicts this ongoing confusion. Every Easter, a Baptist church in Wilmington, NC gathers to proclaim Jesus' resurrection. Oddly enough, this church holds its Easter worship on the decks of a battleship. At this battleship Easter service, there are other strange juxtapositions: a U.S. flag hangs draped over the cross; in addition to singing hymns, the church says the Pledge of Allegiance; as the worshippers' faces turn east towards the dawn light to greet their Lord's resurrection, the "faces" of bristling large-bore deck guns also face east, ominously standing guard against "the enemy." What, one might ask, do all these armaments have to do with the worship of Jesus Christ?

This very real situation (my neighbor grew up in this church) may seem an anomaly; yet I believe it symbolizes the unacknowledged alliance with Empire that plagues the church in North America. In this country the cross and the battleship, the Christian story and the American story, have become nearly inseparable. We have become a church of "battleship believers"—while our Easter liturgy sings praise to Jesus, Prince of Peace, our swivel-action deck guns point to Mars, god of war. The church, in the words of poet and farmer Wendell Berry, "has become willy-nilly the religion of the state and the economic status quo...it has flown the flag and chanted the slogans of empire." Our tacit, even explicit support of America's militarism results in this unspoken-but-all-too-clear message: *we believe that Jesus is Lord, but we don't believe it enough to renounce our country's power and violence. We've got Jesus to protect our hearts, but to protect our shores, our homeland, and our "national interests," we're armed with battleships, smart bombs, and the 82nd Airborne Division.*

If my characterization seems overblown or far-fetched, we need only flip through a few back issues of *The Christian Cen-*

tury or *Christianity Today* to read about the widespread Christian support of the past three wars in the Middle East (not to mention all the other wars our country has waged in its relatively short life span).

How have we steered so far off course? One of the main reasons the church bows to this kind of militaristic idolatry is that we've failed to see that the kingdom of God is a political reality. Our truncated gospel preached on any given Sunday tells us that the kingdom of God is located either in our hearts or at the end of time. But this completely misses the message of the New Testament.

The Gospels make it clear that Jesus' kingdom has already begun. His kingdom is both an alternative and an affront to the world-as-we-know-it. It cannot be confined to the realms of the heart or to some distant future. It is a whole new way of living in the world—an entirely new creation (II Cor.5:17).

The group Jesus gathered—first his disciples, later the early church—continued to embody the kingdom of God, becoming what New Testament scholar Gerhard Lohfink calls a "contrast-society," a society living in—but distinct from—the world. This new society dealt with the problem of possessions by sharing them; it welcomed the stranger, the widow, the orphan. It dealt with enemies by loving them, even dying at their enemy's hand as their Lord had.

Jesus' contrast-society was a *polis,* a new political reality. And the politics Jesus left with his disciples were specific regarding how they should treat each other, their neighbors, and their enemies. In Matthew's Sermon on the Mount (and parallels in Luke 6), Jesus tells his disciples, "You have heard it said, 'you shall love your neighbor and hate your enemy.' But I say to you, Love your enemies and pray for those who persecute you, so that you may be children of your Father in heaven;…be perfect, therefore, as your father in heaven is perfect" (Matt 5:43-45a; 48). Jesus makes it clear that these teachings are to be put into practice (Matt. 7:24-27; Luke 6:46-49). At the end of Matthew's Gospel, in what is often called "The Great Commission," Jesus tells his followers: "Go therefore and make disciples of all nations, baptizing them in the name of the Father, and of the Son, and of the Holy Spirit, and *teaching them to obey everything that I have commanded you* (italics mine). No small feat, considering everything Jesus taught in Matthew's Gospel. Included in that "everything" is the command to love our enemies, to be active peacemakers.

The church has been quite creative in its attempts to squirm out from under Jesus' commands in the Sermon on the Mount, building elaborate scaffolds of interpretation to explain why Jesus doesn't really mean what he says. Dietrich Bonhoeffer, the martyred German pastor and theologian, offered a corrective: "Humanly speaking, we could interpret the Sermon on the Mount in a thousand different ways. Jesus knows only one possibility: simple surrender and obedience. He does not want it to be discussed as an ideal; he really means us to get on with it."

We have the Sermon on the Mount, but more importantly, we have the enactment of the sermon in the person of Jesus Christ. The striking thing is that Jesus didn't just preach *about* the peaceable kingdom of God, he *embodied* that kingdom. Jesus' life, death, and resurrection *is* a whole new social ethic for the people of God. We see Jesus embody this ethic of nonviolent enemy love most completely on the cross, for the cross is how God showed his love for his own enemies. Paul says in Romans 5:10, "For if while we were enemies, we were reconciled to God through the death of his Son, much more surely, having been reconciled, will we be saved by his life."

The New Testament writers tell us that the cross must determine the shape of our own lives as well. *Cruciformity* is the inescapable pattern of existence for those who would follow Jesus Christ. When we refuse to live as cruciform peacemakers, our proclamation of the gospel—God's peace-treaty with the world—becomes so much religious gibberish. We cannot proclaim Jesus' resurrection from the decks of battleships. If we support an Empire that slaughters Iraqi children in the name of "freedom," we are not simply supporting the right cause with the wrong means—we are betraying the gospel.

Active enemy-love is a command from Jesus, but that doesn't

mean that it's one more rule to follow. Rather, it's a whole new way of living in the world, because our lives become a sign of our *eschatological hope*. The New Testament depicts this hope vividly in the book of Revelation. The apocalyptic message John sends to the churches in Asia Minor is that Jesus the Slaughtered Lamb has already triumphed, and that his kingdom has already broken into our world. A loud voice in heaven tells John, "The kingdom of the world has become the kingdom of our Lord and of his Messiah, and he will reign forever and ever" (Rev. 11:15-18).

Written during a time of persecution, the refrain echoing throughout Revelation is that those in the church are to have patience and endurance (Rev. 6:9-11; 13:10; 14:12). The posture the saints assume in Revelation is that of the Lamb—suffering obedience. John tells us that when the saints met evil they conquered it not through force, but by "the blood of the Lamb and by the word of their testimony, for they did not cling to life even in the face of death" (12:11). Speaking of the Revelation's call to nonviolence John H. Yoder says, "The church's suffering, like the Master's suffering, is the measure of the church's obedience to the self-giving love of God. Nonviolence is right, in the deepest sense, not because it works, but because it anticipates the triumph of the Lamb that was slain."

To follow Jesus' nonviolent way in a world wracked by violence and strife is to choose a costly path. Because of sin we all have violence deep within us. Though I know what I *should* do, I can't claim to know how I would respond if someone attacked me or my family. But I do know that the kind of questions with which I began only distract from the kind of imaginative discipleship to which our Lord calls us. We need no longer ask if it's permissible for Christians to kill, because the searing light of the gospel has shown us a different way to treat our enemies. We need not hear the siren call that seduces us onto battleships, we need not drink the poisoned water of our country's bitter wars, for our Lamb calls us to live in a different kingdom, to drink from a different well:

The Spirit and the bride say,
  "Come."
And let everyone who hears say,
  "Come."
And let everyone who is thirsty
  come.
Let anyone who wishes take the
  water of life as a gift.

—Rev.22:17

Conflict Resolution

If another member of the church sins, go and point out the fault when the two of you are alone. If the member listens to you, you have regained that one. (Matt. 18:15)

So far my discussion has centered on our posture towards the enemy "out there." But how do we make peace with "the enemy" within our own church? When conflict comes between members of the body of Christ, as it unavoidably does, how do we deal with it? Jesus foresaw the inevitability of conflict within the church, and in Matthew 18 he gave his followers a set of guidelines for how to deal with it.

The purpose of speaking to an errant brother or sister is to "regain" him or her, to restore that person to the fellowship, to reconcile that person back to the body of Christ. This way of dealing with conflict looks very different from the way the world works. The primary aim of the American prison system, for example, is *punishment*, not restoration. But punishing a wrong-doer is not the aim of Matthew 18. The goal Jesus gives the church is to forgive and to restore.

If after the initial confrontation the wayward member doesn't listen to you, Jesus says, take one or two more members along with you. If the member still won't listen to you, bring the matter before the whole church. Jesus recognized that the propensity for human error is such that it may take the whole church confronting a brother or sister in error before they repent. And if they still won't repent? "If the offender refuses to listen even to the church," Jesus says, "let such a one be to you as a Gentile and a tax collector" (v.17). But what does that mean? Most would interpret Jesus as saying, "If they still won't listen, boot 'em!", which has been the justification for the church using excommunication. But yet Jesus still chose to eat with Gentiles and tax collectors, even though they were reviled, which complicates any attempt to simply kick out the offender.

My fellow church member Jen Graber, while preaching on this passage, took a different tact. "How do we treat the Gentile and the tax collector, the one in error who refuses to listen?" Jen asked. "We keep going to dinner at their house!"—in other words, we keep trying to reconcile with them and return them to our fellowship.

The parallel story in John 20 is striking. In John's account, Jesus' mandate to forgive is inseparably linked with the coming of the Holy Spirit. Jesus breathes the Holy Spirit on his disciples, and immediately after tells them, "If you forgive the sins of any, they are forgiven them; if you retain the sins of any, they are retained." According to John's Gospel, the church's authority to forgive is inextricably linked with the gift of the Holy Spirit. It is only through the Holy Spirit that we are able to do the hard work of forgiveness and reconciliation. To be active peacemakers, we all need a community that both holds us accountable and trains us to live lives of cruciform discipleship. In the midst of a church that has bowed to the gods of nationalism and militarism, where will we find such communities? Perhaps the following stories can set fire to our imaginations.

III. Active Peacemaking in New Monastic Communities

The Bruderhof—"We must dare to be open"

Jutta Manke, a member of a Christian community called the Bruderhof, recounts a conflict that arose in the kindergarten where she works. The head teacher, it seems, had turned into a dictator, bossing around the other teachers and exerting her power irresponsibly. Jutta and the other teachers remained quiet, hoping things would improve on their own. Surprised that one of her own sisters in Christ could behave this way, Jutta remarked, "Hadn't we found a community of brothers and sisters who had renounced all power over people and every form of violence in order to follow the way of love and of mutual subordination? We had been fascinated by the atmosphere of peace we had sensed everywhere. And now *this!*"

Jutta and the other teachers continued to put up with the bossy director, still in denial that this could be happening. Jutta could not "vent" about this to her husband; when she joined the Bruderhof, she agreed not to talk behind anyone's back. The Bruderhof had structured its community along the lines of Matt. 18: if you have a problem, first address the person who has wronged you. Finally one of the other teachers did just that. She asked that all the teachers talk about the "un-peaceful atmosphere" in their Children's House.

To Jutta's surprise, the bossy and domineering sister soon "began to speak concretely about her own sin and failure." But the bigger surprise came when Jutta realized her own part in her sister's sin. By refusing to speak truth to her sister in error, she was complicit as well.

She realized it was not just a problem with her sister, but "was also a matter of my sin—my unbelief and my lack of trust that with the Spirit of God things really could be completely different among us human beings."

The sisters were reconciled, using "the community's God-given authority to cast confessed sin into the depths of the sea." The peace that resulted for these Bruderhof women was the reward for the hard business of confronting the one in error. This peace, says Jutta, "is possible if we open the door to one another in love and commitment. Voluntary commitment is the foundation of every relationship. If there is to be peace, we must dare to be open!"

The Rutba House—Hospitality as Peacemaking

How can we witness against our country's war-making? This was the question that drove Leah and Jonathan Wilson-Hartgrove to Iraq at the onset of the U.S. attacks in March 2003. They went with a group from Christian Peacemaker Teams, an ecumenical violence-reduction initiative that sends teams to war zones around the world as peace witnesses. But hearing Jonathan and Leah tell the story, it was they themselves who received the witness, learning a lesson in peacemaking from a most unlikely source.

Their team arrived in Baghdad on March 24th, just seven days after the U.S. began its bombing campaign. On the morning of their fourth day, after visiting bombed houses, shops, and civilian areas, the Iraqi police arrested their group for traveling without supervision. The police said they had to leave the country.

Nearly half-way between Baghdad and their destination in Amman, Jordan, the group realized that the rear car carrying CPT members Cliff Kindy, Weldon Nisly, and Shane Claiborne was missing. Eventually they turned around and drove back towards Baghdad. They soon found the third car on the side of the road, one of its tires blown, blood covering the windshield and seats. Their team members were gone.

They drove to the closest town to look for their friends, to a place called Rutba (pronounced "Root-ba"). "When we got to Rutba, we asked where the hospital was," Jonathan said. "We were told that the U.S. had bombed it."

They went to a makeshift clinic in town and found their friends. The Iraqi doctor tending to their friends' broken bones told them, "Three days ago your country bombed our hospital. But don't worry, whether you're American or Iraqi, Christian or Moslem, we will take care of you, because we take care of everybody." Before the group departed for Jordan, they asked the doctor, "What do we owe you?" "Nothing," the doctor replied, "Just go home and tell the people of the world what happened in Rutba."

They did. When the team finally arrived in Amman, they told the story first to the UN, then to every major news media group in the world. They were the first internationals to confirm that the

U.S. had bombed the civilian hospital in Rutba.

But not everyone wanted to hear the story. Before returning to the U.S., Shane, Leah and Jonathan planned to stop off in New York at the request of CNN to do an interview. The anchor-woman called them in Amman to do a 'pre-interview'. She spoke with Shane, and after a few minutes of asking him questions, she said, "Wait, let me get this right. You're telling me that the Iraqi people did not want this war?" "That's correct," Shane said, confirming what the group had heard in many conversations with Iraqis.

There was a pause on the line. The CNN anchor-woman said, "I'm going to have to talk with my producer about this. I'll get back with you." She didn't call back, and CNN never aired the story.

"We realized," Jonathan told me, "that the story of 'the enemy' extending hospitality to Americans after our country had bombed them was too disturbing a thing for American TV viewers to hear. The culture of hospitality we saw in the Rutba hospital ran so counter to the culture of war portrayed by the media, that the Rutba story simply couldn't be told. The story of war that CNN, Fox, NBC—all the major media outlets—were telling, was about *us* against *them*. We were telling a story about *them* helping *us*, and the media wouldn't touch it. We realized that hospitality is subversive. It goes against the grain. Hospitality is really a form of peacemaking, because it blurs the boundaries between *us* and *them*."

Rather than returning to Baghdad, Leah and Jonathan decided that they would try and emulate the hospitality they had received in Rutba. They moved to Durham, NC and, along with Isaac Villegas, opened a hospitality house in an urban neighborhood, welcoming "the enemy"—prisoners, drug addicts, the homeless—into their home.

Following the request of the Iraqi doctor, they named their community "Rutba House." Whenever someone asks, "Rutba? What's Rutba?", Jonathan, Leah or Isaac will grin and say, "Well, let me tell you the story."

Las Abejas—"Our weapon is the Word of God"

In the spring of 2001 I traveled to Chiapas, Mexico with Christian Peacemaker Teams as a peace worker. Since 1994, the Mexican government had waged a U.S.-sponsored low-intensity war against its own citizens. The government claimed that some "Marxist revolutionaries" from Cuba had infiltrated the ranks of their hard-working peasant farmers and convinced them to take up arms. The reality was that the farmers were tired of a government that denied them the services that every government should provide: a decent education, a living wage, and respect for one's cultural and religious practices.

After repeated demands for justice, a desperate group of these peasant farmers calling themselves the Zapatistas took up arms. They mounted a small revolution, lasting only twelve days, and then called for dialogues. With the official fighting over and dialogues underway, the Mexican government—with help from the U.S.—began its low-intensity war designed to spread fear among the civilian population and to deter potential Zapatista recruits. The government began training paramilitary groups, armed vigilantes who were paid to terrorize and kill anyone suspected of being a Zapatista supporter.

Our team worked with a group of indigenous Christians calling themselves *Las Abejas*. Though they had been attacked by paramilitaries, the *Abejas* rejected the armed path of the Zapatistas, choosing instead Jesus' way of nonviolence. They had simply read Jesus' words in the Sermon on the Mount, and said "we've got to live this way; this is what our Lord commands."

When I asked one of them how they came to call themselves *Las Abejas*, meaning "the Bees," a man named Antonio smiled and said, "We are like bees because we are a community that works together for the common good; we have a queen, which is the kingdom of God. And like bees, we have a sting. But our sting is not a weapon made by human hands; our weapon is the Word of God."

This decision came with a price. On December 22nd, 1997, over 100 paramilitaries descended upon the tiny village of Acteal, where a group of *Abejas* had spent the past three days praying and fasting for peace. The paramilitaries opened fire on a crowd of worshippers, and spent the next six hours hunting down men, women, and children. Forty-five *Abejas* were killed, as they offered no resistance. According to survivors, one *Abejas* man prayed aloud Jesus' words during the massacre: "Father, forgive them for they know not what they do."

Fearing another attack many *Abejas* became *desplazados*, displaced people, forced to leave their homes and land. They resolved to stand firm in their nonviolent witness, trusting in God's ultimate justice rather than taking up arms against their enemies. Three years ago, some of the Abejas were able to sit down with members of the paramilitary group, the same ones who had killed their brothers and sisters, and forgive them.

Las Abejas are a neo-monastic community in a number of ways, but their nonviolent witness, their trusting God enough to die rather than meet evil on its own terms, is their most powerful witness to the American church. Along with Paul, they know what it means "to know Christ and the power of his resurrection and the sharing of his sufferings by becoming like him in his death" (Phil. 3:10).

Mark 12: Commitment to a Disciplined Contemplative Life

Jonathan Wilson-Hartgrove

I. A Personal Story

For the record: I am not a very good contemplative. If I am in any way qualified to write on the contemplative life in the new monasticism, it is because of my friendship with Jim Douglass that began in the western desert of Iraq. My wife Leah and I, along with Jim and other Christian peacemakers, were being driven east from Jordan through a terrible dust storm to Baghdad. Seven days into Operation Iraqi Freedom, the city was under siege. Our goal was to join the Iraq Peace Team, a group of about 35 men and women who had remained in Baghdad as bombs began to fall, praying for peace and standing with those who could not leave their homes. Joining them was my attempt to "do something" when protests in the United States seemed futile.

The only cars we passed on the road to Baghdad were charred frames with their doors standing open, as if their passengers had made one last attempt to jump before a missile hit. Already the blowing dust was beginning to cover these skeletons of iron. At one point on the road, we saw a car still burning up ahead of us. Our driver slowed to pass through the cloud of black smoke. I watched anxiously to see what was on the other side. Three men

162

stood in the road, guns at their feet with their hands in the air. They were facing a hill where we looked to see U.S. troops standing outside their Humvees with M-16s pointed in our direction. One of the soldiers motioned for our driver to stop. He did. My eyes scanned the hillside as I counted men and guns and armored vehicles. Leah stared back at the scope of a machine gun. On the other end was a soldier, staring at us. Neither of us could do anything. Our lives in the hands of nervous nineteen year-olds, Leah and I froze. It was, for me, the end of activism as I had known it. In the desert I had to face the reality that in our struggle against war and injustice, there are times when we can do nothing.

Beside me, though, was Jim Douglass. I did not look at him until after the troops had realized that their Iraqi captives were running to jump on our vehicle and hurriedly waved us on. Jim was writing in a notebook, patiently describing the scene as it unfolded. Minutes before Leah had asked Jim if he thought we were safer because of the dust storm blocking visibility from the air. "If they want us, they can find us," Jim had said. Noticing the worry on Leah's face, he smiled: "But God will take care of us." God had. And Jim, so far as I could tell, had never blinked.

What is it about some people that tells you when you look at them that God is there? I'm not sure. Just the other day an older gentleman from my home church was telling me about his late father, whom I never met. "If ever there was a saint that walked this earth, it was him," he said. That's the feeling I get when I think of Jim (though I wouldn't call him a saint. As Dorothy Day, co-founder of the Catholic Worker movement, used to say, I don't want to dismiss him so easily.) Meeting Jim at just the moment when I'd reached the end of activism opened my eyes to the importance of a contemplative life.

Just five days after our journey into Baghdad, Leah and I were arrested by Iraqi police officers and given less than 24 hours to leave the country. The next morning, before we set out to travel once more across that perilous desert, Jim led our peace team in a devotion. He shared with us how his friend Thomas Merton had taught him to pray, encouraging him to abandon his entire self to the unknown and to trust that God would catch him. Such prayer is a discipline. But we do not practice it alone. Because "Tom," as Jim called him, was a member of the eternal communion of saints, he could pray for us. On our journey through the desert, Jim assured us that Tom would be praying.

As we were leaving I asked Jim if he would be my Thomas Merton—if he would teach me to pray as Tom had taught him. Jim paused. "Well, let's see. If you ask me, I could ask Tom, and he could ask God…. Yes, I think that would work." With that, I gained both a spiritual director and a new perspective on what it means to have a relationship with Jesus and his body, the church. Over the past year and a half I have begun a journey into the contemplative life with the help of Jim and Thomas Merton. What I have to offer here is only beginner's wisdom—a sense that the new monasticism cannot survive without becoming rooted in the disciplines of a contemplative life. Just what this will mean we must discover together. For now, I'd like to share some of what I've learned from Jim and Tom about what the contemplative life is and why it is so important. I'll conclude with some stories about what contemplation looks like in the lives of people who are living this new monasticism.

II. Resistance and Contemplation in Scripture and Tradition

St. Ambrose wrote that "all who wish to return to paradise must be tested by fire." Only by passing through the fire—what Merton called the "flaming sword at the gates of Eden"—can we know liberation. In his book *Resistance and Contemplation*, Jim observes that the liberation movements of the past century recognized one dimension of the truth that Ambrose articulates. Only by suffering the fires of resistance can a people gain freedom. This is as true of nonviolent resistance movements as it is of violent liberation struggles. Those schooled in Scripture, however, must recognize that there are two dimensions of liberation: freedom from social oppression and freedom from the sin which is the root of social oppression. Resistance is the fire in which we find freedom from social oppression. Contemplation is the flame through which our own souls find liberation.

Too often we fail to recognize these two dimensions of what it means to be "set free." Conservatives have traditionally focused solely on the personal conversion of individuals, not recognizing the importance of social institutions and the degree to which their structures are in need of redemption. Liberals, on the other hand, have often critiqued and fought against racism, classism, sexism, and militarism without acknowledging how they themselves are inevitably complicit in these social evils. The result is that we have together failed to hear the entirety of Jesus' call: "Repent, for the kingdom of God is near."

True repentance is the beginning of contemplation. The Greek word for "repentance" in the New Testament may be translated literally as "change of mind." It is a confession that even the way we think about the world as fallen creatures is wrong. Because we do not think right, it is not possible for us to act right. To have a "change of mind" is to learn to see the world differently. By God's grace, we learn to see as God sees—that is, to see the world as it truly is. This does not happen all at once. It takes a long time. A person may be converted in a moment, baptized and sealed by the Holy Spirit as one who belongs to the family of God before she leaves the church building. What the theologians call "perfection," however, takes a lifetime. Receiving the gift of the "mind of Christ" is a lot of work. The name that the Christian tradition gives for that work is "contemplation."

Because of the division in the church that followed the Reformation, it is important for me to pause here and make clear what I mean by the "work" of contemplation. A practice such as this which has been passed down through the Catholic tradition may be criticized by some Protestants as "works righteousness" or an attempt to "earn our salvation." Protestants are often cautious when they hear someone say that perfection requires work. After all, Jesus saves us once and for all by his redeeming work on the cross. The most Protestant of Protestants, however, agrees on this point: we are co-laborers with God in the re-formation of our own lives. Yes, only God can save us. And only God can make us fit for heaven. But just as we must accept God's gift of grace for salvation, we must also participate in the process of our being made holy. We must work to see the world as God sees it.

Scripture shows us what this work looks like when done well in the story of Jesus' temptation in the wilderness. Because Jesus was in every way God, we know that he had the mind of Christ. He did not have to work for it. It was part of who he was as the Son of God. Because Jesus was also fully human, though, he had a human imagination. Though he was without sin, Jesus had to do the work of contemplation to train his brain in faithful patterns of thought and action. The Gospels tell us that Jesus did this often, leaving the disciples to pray by himself (e.g. Mark 6:46). In the story of Jesus' temptation in the wilderness, we get a glimpse of what this work looks like.

Jesus' temptation follows the story of his baptism in all of the Gospel accounts. A voice from heaven speaks to say, "This is my beloved Son in whom I am well pleased." Immediately, Mark's Gospel says, the Spirit drove Jesus out into the wilderness. Why the wilderness? Why do the abandoned and desolate places play so importantly in the life of contemplation? Because this is where the devil reigns. Wilderness and water serve as symbols in Scripture to represent the chaos that is always lurking at the fringes of God's good creation. Jesus goes out into the wilderness because he is going to do spiritual battle on the devil's turf. Contemplation is not about a "quiet time" when we can feel safe with God. In contemplation we learn to trust God precisely because we need him.

Without bread, water, bed, or companion, Jesus can hear nothing but the noise of the devil's temptations. They are temptations he must learn to resist now, for they will be with him throughout his ministry. "Turn these stones into bread," Satan says. There are two dimensions to the temptation: Jesus is hungry and, like Esau, is tempted to sell his birthright for a simple meal. That is the personal struggle. On the social level, Jesus will soon face hungry crowds that are more than ready to make him their king if he will only turn the stones into bread and feed them (John 6:15). In the wilderness Jesus resists the temptation he will soon face to seize economic power by feeding the masses. He is disciplining his mind and body to follow a different way. Twice more the devil will tempt him: once to take hold of political power and rule over all the nations of the earth; once to throw himself from the temple and become a "wonder worker." Each time Jesus rejects the way of the devil, insisting with Scripture that God has another way. In the wilderness Jesus is choosing the way of the cross.

Contemplation is about learning to see the world through the lens of the cross. It is a simple confession of the Christian faith that Jesus went to the cross, died for our sins, and calls us to take up our own crosses to follow him. Christians believe that. But to live your whole life as if that were true—that is something that has to be learned. Mother Teresa is often cited as an example from the 20th century of one who lived a Christ-like life. You don't even have to be a Christian to see that she lived according to the Sermon on the Mount and the teachings of Jesus. Thousands of preachers hold her life up as an example for their congregations. Rarely, however, do I hear anyone explain the years of contemplation that Mother Teresa practiced in order to become the kind of person who could serve as Christ served. For most of us in our daily lives, the way of the cross still seems like a bad idea. Sure, it is a wonderful thing that Jesus died for us. Choosing to die for my enemies, though, is not something I'm hardwired to do. Mother Teresa learned to see the world differently. After years of adoring her crucified Savior in contemplation, she became the kind of person who could love denying herself for her neighbor's sake. She did not serve the poor because they made her feel guilty. She lived among the poorest of the poor as a humble servant because she could not imagine a better life. She had experienced a "change of mind." Mother Teresa had received the mind of Christ.

Contemplation is the way Christ has opened for us to receive his mind—to learn to see, as the Mennonite theologian John Yoder said, that "those who carry crosses work with the grain of the universe." But this way of contemplation is not a technique. Contemplation is not a skill that we can perfect so as to ensure the right result. Perfection in contemplation is the realization that we do not know what we are doing. The cross does not break life's secret code, giving us all the right answers. To have the mind of Christ is to know that the cross can only look like a disaster from the front-side. "My God, my God, why have you forsaken me?" (Mt.27:46), Jesus prays before the cross. We cannot pretend to see any more than this when we face our own crosses. But we can trust God. We can believe that the darkest darkness may indeed be a light so bright that it is blinding our weak eyes. We can believe that beyond death there is resurrection. "Into thy hands I commend my spirit." This is the prayer of the contemplative. We must work hard to learn to pray it without ceasing. But none of us can pray it even once without God's help. "Into thy hands I commend my spirit," is a prayer that Jesus speaks through us.

III. Stories of Neo-monastic Contemplation

Jim Douglass

As I've already said, most of what I know about contemplation I learned from Jim. His books have been invaluable resources as I stumble along toward a more contemplative life. Contemplation would not matter nearly as much to me, though, if I had not seen the difference it makes in Jim's life. I'm glad to be able to tell part of his story as an example of the contemplative life in the new monasticism.

Jim lives in a little hermitage by the train tracks in Birmingham, Alabama. In the language of so many Southern towns, his house is on the "wrong side of the tracks." Jim and his wife, Shelley, moved there to "watch and pray" over an economically depressed neighborhood and the trains that carried weapons-grade nuclear material through it. In recent years those trains have stopped traveling; the U.S. government found better means of transportation. So Jim and Shelley started Mary's House, a Catholic Worker house across town that welcomes families who have fallen through the cracks of welfare reform. Jim, however, still spends most of his time at the "Tracks House," pursuing a contemplative life in writing and prayer. Each morning he rises early to read a few verses of Scripture from the Greek New Testament. It's a practice his Muslim friends shamed him into, Jim says, because they insist on *always* reading their Scriptures in their original language of Arabic. Reading in the original languages slows Jim down. He likes that. After reading, Jim prays in silence. He insists that he doesn't really know how to do it, but quotes a Buddhist hermit who lives in a cave above a river in rural British Columbia as saying, "Prayer is listening with God's ears." Those ears are a gift that it takes a long time to receive. Jim has them.

Like Thomas Merton, Jim believes that writing is prayer—or it should be. Jim writes slowly, drafting once on a legal pad and often twice on his typewriter before typing a final draft into the computer. Books, then, come slowly. Especially because Jim thinks his personal correspondence is more important work than his books. In his letters, Jim prays contemplatively, asking the Holy Spirit to help him say what the reader—the single reader—needs to hear. In this practice there is a recognition of the fact that every human being is a wonder, created in God's image and deserving special attention. Jim practices a hospitality of the pen which is, as Dorothy Day said, "hospitality of the heart." I know all this not because Jim told me, but because I am a grateful recipient of the fruits of his contemplation.

Weldon Nisly

After a long day of fruitless protest in Washington, D.C., Weldon Nisly slumped down in the back row of a worship service at the Sojourners community in Columbia Heights. He had come to the end of his rope. After years of trying to work for peace and justice, Weldon's energy was gone and he saw little reason for hope. Not even in the church. As the worship service moved toward a celebration of communion, he resolved to not even go forward. It could not help. He wanted out. Then, in an experience that he can only describe as mystical, Weldon had a vision of Christ calling him to the table to eat and be nourished. His life and faith were changed. In a way he could not see before, Weldon now saw the risen Christ in the broken bread as the two disciples saw the risen Jesus in Emmaus (Luke 24:31). In this encounter Weldon knew in an entirely new way the "profound mystery and reality of the Eucharist as the center of life and faith—and the unity of prayer and peace."

Weldon's vision of Christ led him to become a pastor in his own tradition, the Mennonite Church. In that role as spiritual leader, he was able to offer others the body and blood of Christ while proclaiming the good news that Jesus had shared with him. Because of his desire to deepen his roots in the contemplative life, Weldon also became a Benedictine oblate—that is, a follower of the monastic rule of St. Benedict who lives outside the monastery. (He is a member of the Bridgefolk group that Ivan described in chapter five.) As Mennonite pastor and Benedictine oblate, Weldon seeks to understand how the Lord's Supper can lead Christians into lives of resistance and contemplation. Weldon's life is a beautiful example of what that pursuit can look like. It means respectfully refusing to pay war taxes to the IRS, engaging in nonviolent direct action with the Christian Peacemaker Teams, and fostering interfaith dialogue about Christian-Muslim relations in Seattle. It also means living a few weeks of each year with the monks at St. Johns Abbey in Collegeville, Minnesota, where he is an oblate, praying the hours in his daily life, and working to create a rule of life that is fully Mennonite and fully Benedictine. For Weldon the two tasks of cultivating a deeper spirituality and engaging the world have become one. It is all action. And it is all contemplation.

Prisoners of Conscience

Despite her protests against the policies of the U.S. government, Dorothy Day always insisted that "Holy Mother the State" could be an instrument of the Lord to guide us toward faithfulness. For hundreds of committed Christians in recent years, prison has become a "new monastery" where resistance and contemplation converge. Carol Gilbert, O.P., is but one example. She and two other Dominican sisters were arrested in 2003 for trespassing on a nuclear weapons facility in Colorado where they had gone to pray for peace. Now Carol is prisoner # 10856-039 at the Federal prison camp in Alderson, WV. There she is forced to keep a disciplined schedule in which she keeps hours praying, writing letters, eating, and doing simple tasks with her hands. As in the ancient monasteries, she is removed from the distractions of daily life and forced to practice stability in one of the abandoned places of our society. Inside the prison her perspective is changed; she sees America from the underside, forced to face her own deep darkness. But hers is a gospel story, for God meets her there in her prison cell. The following prayer sent to friends in February of 2004 is a testimony to her contemplative life:

> Close your eyes and you will see clearly.
> Cease to listen and you will hear truth.
> Be silent and your heart will sing.
> Seek no contact and you will find union.
> Be still and you will move forward in the tide of the Spirit.
> Be gentle and you will not need strength.
> Be patient and you will achieve all things.
> Be humble and you remain entire.

My Journey at Rutba House

Every morning I try to wake up thirty minutes before I have to do anything or go anywhere. I brush my teeth, make a cup of tea, and stumble into the little prayer nook that we have under our stairs. I light three candles, sit upright in a wooden chair, steady my breathing, and sit there. I haven't figured out just how to do it, but I try to focus on God. Some days I repeat the name of Jesus over and over again. Some days I pray the Jesus prayer: "Lord Jesus, Son of God, have mercy on me a sinner." We have a rosary on the desk. I don't know how to pray it, but I roll my thumb over the beads some mornings. I try to give myself to God. Usually I end up thinking about someone I need to talk to or a project I'm working on or the book I was reading when I fell asleep the night before. When I catch myself, I try to focus on the chant again: "Jesus, Jesus,

Jesus...." Inevitably, my mind wanders again. This bothered me a great deal until I read Teresa of Avila who told me that I need not fight against those thoughts, but should let them wash over me, rejoicing in the truth that God is an anchor who can hold me even in the storms of my mind. I'm not very good at contemplation. But contemplation is not about me. It's about God.

Contemplation is something that I experience alone, in the early morning hours of the day. Lately, however, I have been learning a new sort of mysticism from my brothers and sisters at the St. John's Missionary Baptist Church. When we gather together every Sunday to sing the spirituals of the black church tradition, I am increasingly aware that the experience is much like my time with God in quiet contemplation. The music is repetitive. Over and again we repeat a line: "In the name of Jesus, In the name of Jesus...." Those stanzas become a mantra. I am called to consider God, to focus all of my attention on the glory of the Lord. Here, too, my mind wanders. But the music still washes over me. God is still faithful. And I realize my utter dependence upon God in the company of friends. Together we confess the deep darkness that is within each of us and the social evil that sin creates. Together we proclaim a new creation in the kingdom of God. Indeed, together we *become* a new reality, God's people in the world.

This summer a young man was killed in our neighborhood during a drug related shoot-out. The police came and went, but the neighborhood was still held captive by fear. So the church decided to take to the streets. Every Saturday morning we gather on the corner where the drug dealers hang out. (There are more of us than there are of them.) We split up into groups and canvass the neighborhood, singing as we go and stopping to pray with anyone who'll join us. After an hour, we all return to our starting point, make a circle, and sing together. On the street corner, we have church. Activists might call what we do on Saturday mornings a protest. It is. But it is more. It is also contemplation—a corporate communion with the God who is our peace. On our prayer walks the wall between spirituality and activism collapses. Resistance and contemplation are one.

About the Authors

Fred Bahnson is a farmer and writer in Efland, NC.

Jana Bennet is a Ph.D. student in theology at Duke University in Durham, NC.

Michelle Harper Brix is a founding member of The Simple Way in Philadelphia, PA.

Shane Claiborne is a founding member of The Simple Way in Philadelphia, PA.

David Janzen is the coordinator of the Shalom Missions Network and member of Reba Place Fellowship in Evanston, IL.

Ivan Kauffman is a poet and journalist in Washington, D.C.

Maria Russell Kenny is a member of Communality in Lexington, KY.

Sr. Margaret M. McKenna is co-founder of New Jerusalem Now recovery community in Philadelphia, PA.

Chris Rice is co-director of the Center for Reconciliation at Duke Divinity School in Durham, NC.

Sherrie Steiner is an author and teacher in Wayne, PA.

Jon Stock is a publisher at Wipf and Stock, a cooperative enterprise of the Church of the Servant King in Eugene, OR.

Jonathan R. Wilson is Professor of Theology and Ethics at Acadia Divinity College in Wolfville, Nova Scotia.

Jonathan Wilson-Hartgrove is a founding member of the Rutba House in Durham, NC.

Norman Wirzba is Associate Professor of Philosophy at Georgetown College in Georgetown, KY.